BILINGUAL EDUCATION:
EVALUATION, ASSESSMENT
AND
METHODOLOGY

BILINGUAL EDUCATION:

EVALUATION, ASSESSMENT

AND

METHODOLOGY

Edited by

C. J. DODSON

Published on behalf of the
University of Wales
Faculty of Education

CARDIFF
UNIVERSITY OF WALES PRESS
1985

Bilingual education: evaluation, assessment and methodology.
1.   Education, Bilingual—Wales.
2.   Education, Bilingual—Canada.
I. Dodson, C. J.
371.97'09429   LC3736.G6

ISBN   0-7083-0888-0

Printed in Wales by Bridgend Printing Co. Ltd., Bridgend, Mid Glamorgan.

CONTENTS

LIST OF TABLES

INTRODUCTION

THE PAPERS in this volume deal with the Schools Council Projects on bilingual education at primary- and secondary-school levels. The primary-school Project ran from 1968-1975, followed by a two-year aftercare service, whilst the secondary-school Project started in 1974 and ended in 1978.

Two of the papers, the 'Evaluation' by the present Editor and the 'Assessment' by Dr. Eurwen Price, appeared in summary form in *Bilingual Education in Wales, 5-11,* published by Evans/Methuen Educational/Schools Council in 1978. There is still a steady demand for the typescript of the full reports (originally submitted to the Schools Council in 1975 and hitherto unpublished) by those involved in, or wishing to introduce, bilingual education in various parts of the world. It is hoped that this volume will make the full reports more readily available.

A third paper, prepared by Jim Cummins and Fred Genesee, gives an outsider's view of the Schools Council primary-school Project as well as a brief outline of the development of Welsh-medium and bilingual schools in Wales.

The fourth paper, published in Welsh by the Schools Council in 1981, deals with the classroom methodology of the secondary-school Project. Although the Bilingual Method has here been presented as being specifically for secondary-school pupils (age 11 +), it is also suitable, with only minor modifications relating to maturation levels, for junior-school children (age 8-11). The essential features of the Bilingual Method may also be introduced at nursery and infant-school levels (children aged up to 7), and where applied have already resulted in visible improvements in language learning. The aims of the activities embedded in medium- and message-orientated communication are, of course, satisfied here in play activities throughout.

Not only is the Bilingual Method suitable for bilingual education; it is also being used equally successfully for second- and foreign-language learning. Whilst the various activities built into the method must obviously reflect the unique cultural backgrounds of learners in different parts of the world, the *aims* of any activity are universal, as is the need to recognise the various types of

1

communication in learning procedures and apply them at the appropriate moment in the lesson cycle.

In the full 'Evaluation' of the primary-school Project published here, as well as in internal reports between 1970 and 1975, the different types of communicative interactions are still referred to as 'levels of communication'. Professor W. Butzkamm of Aachen Technical University was at the time conducting parallel feasibility studies in the use of the Bilingual Method for foreign-language learning in Germany. Shortly after the submission of the evaluation report, Professor Butzkamm and the Editor coined the now widely-used term 'medium- and message-orientated communication' for the two levels of communication, to show more readily how the various forms of interaction in classroom language-learning relate to the participants' specific speech intentions. It is the teacher's ability to recognise these types of communication and to generate them at the right moment that determines the rate and limit of pupils' second/foreign-language learning development. It should also be stressed that medium- and message-orientated forms of communication reflect extreme forms of interaction at either end of a communicative spectrum encompassing mixtures of both forms in varying proportions.

The 'Evaluation' also includes an analysis of the way a young bilingual child develops both his preferred and second language for any area of experience. To improve his second language he continually takes certain 'short cuts' which are predominantly medium-orientated activities. By doing this he learns how to cope with subsequent message-orientated communicative acts so as to be able to satisfy his immediate non-linguistic needs. These different types of communication and the sequence in which they occur are reflected in the individual steps of the Bilingual Method, which are described in the final paper.

We state categorically that if any 'natural' language-learning is to be replicated for second-language learning in the classroom, language-teaching methods cannot be based on the way a young monolingual child acquires his mother-tongue or a young bilingual child his preferred language, but rather on the way the bilingual child learns and reinforces his second language for any area of experience in his bilingual environment. We are fully aware of the fact that such a proposition requires a total revision of traditional language-teaching and learning theories, including those which form the foundation of the direct method and associated total and continuous monolingual immersion techniques which do not take into account the various levels of communication experienced by the young bilingual (Dodson, 1985, forthcoming).*

The third paper, by Dr. Eurwen Price, an assessment of the Schools Council Project on Bilingual Education in Primary Schools, shows the important finding that bilingual education incorporating the above ideas does not have a detrimental effect on the children's general educational development. The effect of bilingual education on children's general education had been a matter of concern to many people over the years. Dr. Price's findings were therefore received with a sense of relief, especially as the originally monoglot English-speaking pupils also reached a level of communicative competence in Welsh which enabled a significant number of them to enter Welsh-medium secondary schools.

The Centre for Bilingual and Language Education, U.C.W. Aberystwyth, has just completed on behalf of the Welsh Office (the Department of State responsible for Welsh affairs) a research project on the concept development of young monolingual and bilingual children, as well as Welsh learners, who for diverse reasons find themselves in Welsh-medium, English-medium or bilingual schools (report forthcoming). These new findings show that for children in the process of becoming bilingual and for those already bilingual, bilingual education has no detrimental effect on concept development. The results complement Dr. Price's above assessment of children's subject attainment under the same conditions.

These various achievements in bilingual education should give minority-groups everywhere a new sense of hope that all is not irretrievably lost, whilst teachers of foreign languages can approach their difficult tasks with fresh vigour in the knowledge that the majority of their pupils can develop a level of communicative competence in the target language sufficiently high to satisfy the needs of the modern world.

I am very grateful to the Schools Council for giving the Centre for Bilingual and Language Education permission to publish the three reports, and to Jim Cummins and Fred Genesee for their paper comparing the Canadian and Welsh situations. Finally I should like to thank Mrs Sara Thomas for her assistance during the editing of this volume.

C. J. DODSON
JANUARY, 1985

*For references see page 182

Schools Council Bilingual Education Project (Primary Schools) 1968-1977: An Independent Evaluation

C. J. DODSON

THIS INDEPENDENT evaluation based on observations in schools and the test results obtained by Dr. Eurwen Price, Senior Research Officer, is intended not merely for Project teachers and Welsh local authorities, but also for all teachers and authorities in Wales and in other parts of the world where bilingual education might be considered appropriate. The experiences and insights gained in this Project would be of considerable help to those who are faced with the complex task of introducing bilingual education programmes in schools, no matter whether in isolated instances or on a national scale.

The stated aim of the Project was to enable initially monoglot English-speaking children in anglicised areas to achieve, by the end of the primary stage of education, a standard of attainment in Welsh which would give them a sufficiently high degree of English-Welsh bilingualism to cope satisfactorily with everyday living, in and out of school, through the medium of both languages. To achieve this aim the bilingual education programme is introduced at the beginning of state school education, either at reception-class level when children are normally four years of age, or in the first year of the infant school when children are five. The programme continues throughout the child's primary school education, i.e., reception class (age 4), infant school (age 5-7), junior school (age 8-11), until the child is ready for secondary-school education at the age of 11 + . Built into the programme is also the assumption that the equivalent of half the school day is devoted to education where Welsh is used predominantly (English is used during the other half), and that the Welsh sessions should not interfere with the general education and development of the child.

Although the Project did not lay down a detailed methodology taking account of the variables involved in teaching and learning, the first Director of the Project brought with him considerable experience as headmaster of a Welsh-medium primary school with

5

an intake of a large number of monoglot English-speaking children, whilst the majority of Field Officers were recruited from schools already participating in the Project. Additional information was obtained from other schools where individual children had become bilingual at the end of their primary education, whilst further data were obtained from a feasibility study carried out by the Department of Education, the University College of Wales, Aberystwyth, before the project started (Dodson, Price, Williams, 1968).

In this evaluation the various methodological items, either discussed with Project Officers and teachers or observed in Project schools and other experimental situations, will be brought together into a cohesive pattern sufficiently flexible to be used as a basis for the introduction of a bilingual education programme intended for a variety of children in a variety of environments. At the same time difficulties and successes experienced by Project schools will be analysed in relation to this methodological framework.

Being bilingual means that an individual is able to use both languages as a vehicle of communication. He makes use of these languages as a tool with which to satisfy his immediate needs in the process of living. As a rule the bilingual, like the monolingual, is not conscious of language when he makes use of it, because at the time of listening, speaking, reading or writing, his mind is focused on satisfying a variety of immediate needs which in themselves are not linguistic needs. He could be resolving an uncertainty, satisfying his curiosity, making more predictable the unpredictable, clarifying the ambiguous, increasing his pleasure, avoiding pain or unpleasantness, or more generally, solving a problem, executing an activity, acquiring knowledge, or living through a host of other communicative experiences which determine his thought and behaviour patterns as he learns to cope with his environment. In all these processes language is a tool and not an end in itself.

This does not imply, however, that the bilingual individual is able to make use of both languages at the same level of proficiency in all areas of his total range of experience. Bilingualism should not be confused with equilingualism which very few, if any, individuals possess for any length of time and which is certainly not necessary to lead a satisfactory and efficient life in a bilingual community. The bilingual speaker will normally have a preferred language and a second language for different areas of experience, though the status of either of the two languages will depend broadly on which language was used in the initial acquisition of concepts in a given area of experience, the intensity with which these concepts were followed through and the related activities were executed, and the relative amount of contact time with either language in any area of experience. It is, therefore, possible for a bilingual speaker to be operating at preferred- and second-language levels in one area of experience, whilst in another area the status of the two languages is reversed.

Even the very young child who is brought up bilingually will normally have a preferred and a second language. A language becomes a preferred language if (a) the child is able to cope with more aspects of his world in this language and with fewer aspects in the other language and (b) the child feels more 'at home' on a greater number of occasions in one language rather than in the other for those aspects in which he makes use of both languages.

Should the bilingual child be faced with a situation where new concepts and skills are acquired through what to all intents and purposes is the second language, then this language is likely to become the preferred language for that particular range of experience, unless at a later stage this status is reversed because the majority of language contacts in that area is subsequently made in the other language. The development of bilingualism in an individual should thus be considered as an uneven growth process with regard to the status of the two languages, where for any given area of experience at any given time one language is the preferred language and the other the second language, but where one of the languages is not necessarily the preferred languages for *all* areas of experience. Nevertheless, it is possible to classify in general one of these languages as a preferred language and the other as a second language for a child's *total* range of experience according to the definition given above.

It is self-evident that in a bilingual situation the child acquires his second language within those areas of experience into which his preferred language has already become fused to a greater or lesser extent. It should be emphasised at this stage that the child learns his second language areas differently from the way he learnt his equivalent preferred language areas, even though both languages relate to the same range of experience. Whenever he starts to acquire a new range of second language items relating to a particular event he does so by using his preferred language as a point of reference. As his aim is to satisfy as quickly as possible his immediate needs in relation to this event, e.g., to satisfy his curiosity or to increase his pleasure, the child will take a number of shorts-cuts in his second-language acquisition to reach this aim:

(a) If not already offered, he will ask for the preferred-language meaning of words and phrases he cannot understand or about which he is uncertain.

(b) He will repeat to himself or, if acceptable to other children, within a group, words and phrases which he has heard in the second language.

(c) He will compare and contrast utterances with equivalent meanings taken from his preferred and second language.

(d) He will manipulate language by permutating sentence elements in his second language, at times speaking both language versions one after the other or speaking the second-language version after having heard an equivalent preferred-language version.

(e) All the above preliminary processes always occur in what to the child is a situational framework, whether in the child's imagination or in the real world, and not in isolation even though the child's mind may be focused in varying degrees on the second language rather than fully on the situation itself. On many occasions he will 'practise' these processes when by himself after the event.

He will constantly aim to reach a level where he can communicate satisfactorily in order to satisfy his immediate needs (intellectual, physical, emotional, etc.) within an area of experience. In other words, he learns how to cope with his environment mainly by satisfying needs other than those of language, where the second language develops into a tool or vehicle of communication and is not an end in itself. He would not, however, reach this level without the above preliminary steps. It seems that the actual situation, activity or event in which the child finds himself does not afford him a sufficient number of listening and speaking contacts to reach the point where he is no longer aware of making use of his second language. This type of preliminary language 'practising' is constantly being observed in homes where children are being raised bilingually. Examples of this phenomenon will also be given at a later stage when describing the linguistic behaviour of children participating in the Project or the results obtained in schools where these preliminary processes are built into the educational programme or where they are deliberately or unconsciously discouraged. It cannot be stressed too strongly however, that they are *preliminary* processes for any area of experience and that the child's aim is to reach a level where his second language is a tool which no longer impedes, but positively aids, his endeavours to satisfy his total needs.

When a bilingual education programme is introduced, the following points will thus have to be taken into account:

(1) The general methodology should be based on the way a child, brought up bilingually, acquires his second language and not his preferred language. It certainly should not reflect the way in which a monolingual child acquires his mother-tongue. It is for this reason that great care should be taken when methodological concepts such as 'language bath' or 'immediate and total language immersion' are expounded without defining their precise meaning. These concepts should not mean the total exclusion of the preferred language or the mother-tongue, but rather should reflect the way a child in a bilingual country, in an environment where both languages are spoken, learns to acquire or strengthen his second language (a) by referring to his stronger or preferred language and (b) by undergoing the preliminary linguistic short-cuts described above, both during the actual activity and when by himself. Even in those geographical regions where the learner's preferred or first language is hardly ever heard, the child is still subject to these two factors, as is the individual who finds himself in a foreign country whose language he does not know on his arrival.

(2) Just as a child who is already bilingual is motivated to reinforce his second language by his desire to satisfy immediate needs which in themselves are not linguistic needs, so too should a bilingual programme for learners include all those situations, activities and events in which children can satisfy their needs.

(3) These needs should be immediate or at worst short-term, not medium or long-term. The preliminary linguistic short-cuts should themselves take place within a situational framework so that the learner, whilst focusing on language at this stage, can derive immediate satisfaction out of the situation to which this language is attached. Even so-called progressive teaching techniques still tend to create classroom situations where the teacher demands from his pupils stimuli and/or responses (spoken or written) mainly to establish (a) whether the pupil can produce a second or foreign-language stimulus and/or response and (b) whether the stimulus and/or response is a correct one, whilst the pupil's motivation is confined to showing the teacher (or his fellow pupils) that he can in fact produce a correct stimulus or response in the second language.

Whilst the pupil might be rewarded for a correct response, thus satisfying his immediate need for approval, this does not place him in a situation where he can satisfy most of his other needs. This is not to argue that such a need for approval in relation to a correct linguistic response is not important, but great care should be taken to ensure that even during such preliminary work the pupil is also placed into situations where he is allowed and encouraged to focus his mind on the content of the situation so that he can learn 'to make use of' his language as a tool in the exploration of his world.

It is useful to make a distinction between 'using' language and 'making use of' language. The former refers to the process where the pupil focuses mainly on his second-language utterances, whilst the latter refers to the process where the pupil makes use of his language as a tool to satisfy something other than language needs. Both processes refer to communication, but one relates to communication about language whilst the other deals with communication about the real world of which language is only a part. An example of these two levels of communication could be found in a traditional oral language lesson where pupils learn answers to typical questions, e.g., 'How old are you?' In learning to say their answers and the question the pupils are 'using' language to show the teacher that they can in fact say the sentences correctly. This is level 1 communication. As soon as one of the pupils re-directs this question towards the teacher because he wants to know the teacher's age in order to satisfy his curiosity, the focus of the interchange is on something other than language, and language has become a tool. The pupil is 'making use of' language. This is level 2 communication.

In a bilingual education programme all learning procedures should be structured in such a way that the pupil can pass from level 1 to level 2 communication for any activity or topic within an area of experience. It should be emphasised once more, however, that the learner cannot operate immediately at level 2 communication in any new area of experience but must be allowed to reach this level by 'practising' his second language at level 1 within an appropriate activity relating to the particular area of experience. Nevertheless, the constant and most important aim for both pupils and teachers is for *all* learning to evolve into level 2 types of communication. This also implies that at times there is no clear-cut distinction between these two levels in the pupil's mind and that his utterances may well be a mixture of the two levels of communication, however slight his attention to the language may be in a given utterance.

It is also important to note that level 2 communication is not something to be achieved at the end of a few months or years; teachers and pupils should be constantly reaching for it in the course of any unit of work or activity, even right at the beginning of the programme. Making proper use of language has little to do with the range of language acquired at any given time but a great deal to do with the prior ability to manipulate language, no matter how small the range. This is precisely the way a very young bilingual child learns to increase his proficiency in his second language. The various 'practice' steps described earlier, which tend to be level 1 forms of language usage because the child's mind is focused more on the actual language utterances than on satisfying an immediate non-linguistic need, will be dealt with in the context of a bilingual education programme when the Welsh Project is being discussed.

(4) The process is one of constant fluctuation between levels 1 and 2, with both teachers and pupils trying to hold on to level 2 communication for increasing lengths of time, so that eventually most interactions take place at this level, in line with the growing number of activities in interrelated areas of experience which the children have learnt to handle at level 2. Even when communication is at level 1, i.e. the learner's mind is focused on language, no attempt should be made to suppress spontaneous bursts of level 2 communication when these occur; indeed, such bursts should be sustained until the teaching and learning situation demands a return to level 1 work.

(5) Communication at these two levels, especially at level 2, is impossible without allowing the pupils the opportunity of interacting both paralinguistically, that is, by means of 'noises' such as 'Oh!', 'Oh?', 'Ah!', 'Hm!' or 'Mm?', and non-verbally, that is by means of gestures such as wrinkling the brow to show concentration or shrugging the shoulders to show ignorance or lack of concern. Normal communication involves both these forms of interaction, and teachers should therefore structure their classroom procedures to include them. Moreover the pupils should not be permanently desk-bound, since this inhibits paralinguistic and non-verbal behaviour.

(6) Normal communication should take place not only between teacher and pupils but also between pupils themselves.

(7) If pupils are to become bilingual they must be allowed to develop their communicative skills in the second language in relation to all the normal everyday situations encountered by children who share the same environment but for whom this language happens to be the preferred language.

Before starting a bilingual education programme it is wise to investigate the interaction behaviour (linguistic, paralinguistic and non-verbal) of children within the same age-range who already speak the target language, as well as the interaction behaviour of those children who are going to learn the target language. In a bilingual community it could be that the differences in interaction between these two groups of children are slight, although a great deal will depend on the cultural and ethnic composition of the community. It is vitally important, however, to study this interaction behaviour not merely in school, but also outside school and especially in the home. Furthermore, the investigation should cover interaction both between the children themselves, between the children and adults known to them and between the children and strangers, whether adults or other children.

The purpose of such a preliminary investigation would be to ascertain not only the various forms of interaction but also the settings and situations in which these take place. It would then be possible to fuse these factors into the second-language learning procedures of the programme. Without them the children would be learning what to them would be an artificial language which had little bearing on real life and which would generate little or no motivation. Worst of all, the children would never reach a level 2 form of communication, which by definition would deny them the opportunity of becoming bilingual.

(8) It is for these reasons that a bilingual education programme must include areas which relate to the whole range of curricular, extra-curricular and social aspects of the children's experience. Nor should it be limited to the mere linguistic content of these areas of children's experience, as the language to be learnt does not exist in a vacuum but is fused into the interaction processes between individuals and the world in which they live. The child must re-live in terms of the second language those areas he has already experienced through his first language, as well as learn to adjust himself to new areas of experience through both the first and second language. This implies that the interaction processes in the second-language sessions will tend to encompass a wider field of activity than that found in some first-language sessions, especially

in those schools where education is considered to a greater or lesser extent as a self-contained entity, concerned in the main with the teaching of a limited number of skills and a prescribed range of knowledge, but not necessarily closely related to the needs of society outside school.

(9) Once the children are placed in a structured environment conducive to their reaching level 2 communication, care should be taken that the introduction of new concepts embodied in the curriculum of the school is properly phased. At the beginning of the programme, new concepts, especially those which are crucial to the young child's intellectual development, should be introduced during that half of the school day when the mother-tongue is used as a vehicle of communication. Once a concept has been consolidated and proper concept relationships have been formed by means of appropriate activities, this concept can then be further consolidated through new activities in the second-language sessions by relating it to concepts already known in second-language terms. These activities in their turn help the child to form additional concept relationships, giving rise to further second-language stimuli and activities which can spill over once more into the first-language sessions.

Experience has shown that even before the end of the first school year, it is possible to introduce new basic concepts in the second-language sessions. Concepts relating to the development of numeracy, for instance, can be introduced through appropriate second-language activities. Great care should be taken, however, to ensure that the introduction of new concepts in second-language sessions in no way handicaps the child's general development. Should the teacher observe that his class is having difficulty with such a concept because the children have not yet reached a satisfactory level of language comprehension in that area or are not yet able to switch over satisfactorily to level 2 communication for that particular range of activities, then this concept should be introduced during first-language sessions and consolidated in second-language sessions.

The introduction and phasing of concepts across the two languages should thus be viewed as a gradual process. As time progresses and the second language becomes stronger, the number of new concepts introduced during second-language sessions increases.

(10) The ability to switch easily from one language to the other is an important factor in the development of the bilingual child. It has

already been pointed out that the very young child who is brought up bilingually, compares and contrasts utterances from his preferred and second language.

In a school situation the phasing of concepts facilitates this process, since the child switches from one language to the other in relation to the same concepts, which are deliberately re-introduced but in connection with different activities.

(11) All emotional upsets and cases of emergency occurring during the second-language sessions should be settled in the children's mother-tongue, especially in the early stages of the infant school, unless the teacher is absolutely certain that the situation can be resolved in the second language. Teachers are advised to err on the side of caution in this respect as many children will hide their true feeling from their teacher if they realize that, although she may care about their immediate problem, she will not be able to wipe away the trouble because she uses the 'wrong' language. An accumulation of such partially soothed upsets can have devastating long-term effects on a child's personality.

(12) During the preliminary investigation of children's interaction processes (item 7), the type of vocabulary and speech patterns used by children when involved in the variety of daily activities appropriate to their age should be noted and included in the second-language teaching programme. An attempt should be made to grade these language items according to their frequency and difficulty. Obviously the less difficult and the more frequently used speech patterns and vocabulary should occur at the beginning of the programme, although there will always be some conflict between the degree of difficulty and the degree of frequency at which these items occur during the activities. Teachers will thus have to strike a balance, and choose those activities which, whilst furthering children's total development as considered to be necessary by any society, generate linguistic items of high frequency, yet possess a low degree of difficulty. These linguistic factors will also have to be taken into account when deciding upon the phasing of concepts within activity work.

It will not always be possible to exclude some language items considered to be difficult, especially if they are indispensable for some vital activity for which there is no alternative activity available. Rather than reject the activity, and thus interfere with the general development of children, teachers should present such difficult items only in the form in which they appear in that specific activity, and not as a basis for the permutation or manipulation of language elements in order to create new sentences with new meanings for that or any subsequent activities. The time will eventually come when the children reach a language level sufficiently sophisticated to tackle the more difficult parts of language and when they are able to learn how to manipulate even these complex items in the creation of sentences with new meanings.

(13) The manipulation of language, i.e., the substitution of the various sentence elements (vocabulary and parts of sentences) within a speech pattern by using old and new vocabulary in order to create new sentences, is the most important linguistic skill to be learnt by the children. Teachers should, therefore, ensure that pupils receive a great deal of practice in this aspect of language learning. Just as the very young child who is being brought up bilingually outside school, learns this skill of permutating sentence elements in his second language within a situational framework, so too should the school ensure that this preliminary practice for any given range of the child's experience takes place within an activity which is interesting and relevant to him and falls within those activity areas considered necessary for his general development.

These preliminary language activities, which are part of level 1 communication, because the child's mind will be focused partially or wholly on the language rather than on the use he can make of the language in the execution and control of the activity, are the equivalent of drill exercises for older learners. Pure drill work, however, stripped of essential connections with activity work, or worse still, devoid of any situational context, is not suitable at the infant-school level except perhaps for the occasional quick practice for very short periods of a minute or so. But even here such work is best done as part of a language game. The junior-school child, however, being older, can benefit greatly from more intensive practice in the permutation of language elements for periods of up to ten minutes for any drill activity. What is important, however, is that after intensive language work the class is immediately placed into new but related activities where the children can apply and consolidate the language skills and knowledge which they have learnt previously. In other words children should be placed into activity situations where they can learn to reach level 2 communication.

(14) The differences in the rate of second-language acquisition between individual children in the primary school are far greater

than those of secondary-school children, even in mixed-ability classes. This is especially true of infant-school children, whose rate of language acquisition is not merely determined by their various innate linguistic abilities but also by their level of maturation at any given time. Teachers should, therefore, not pre-determine at too early an age a child's linguistic potential, since it is very easy to confuse specific linguistic abilities with levels of maturation. Many young children who are slow starters in the second language in a bilingual education programme blossom forth at a later stage and develop a degree of bilingualism far higher than that of their peers. A child's background and the degree of encouragement he receives outside school is, of course, an additional factor which has to be taken into account (see item 17).

These normal differences in the rate of second-language acquisition between children are a further reason why a primary-school approach, where children are involved in group and individual work, is the only feasible way of allowing children to reach a level of bilingualism of use to the individual and society. Herding young children into school desks where they stay for most of the school day and are taught as a single class, would not only hinder their general intellectual and physical development and their ever attaining true language proficiency related to the real world, but would take no account whatsoever of normal differences in levels of maturation. It should also be pointed out that every young child matures at an uneven rate, so that whilst one child makes rapid strides at one stage and slows down at another, a second child's rate of development might be phased quite differently.

(15) If, on the one hand, pupils can only learn to deal with most facets of life through the second language when they engage in activity work involving level 2 communication, whether verbal or non-verbal, and if, on the other hand, it is required that learners' general development is in no way affected negatively by the second-language learning process, then it is clear that a bilingual programme should be introduced at a stage where activity work is the accepted approach to education. In Britain, as in many other countries, this approach is characteristic of the infant school or reception classes.

There are also neurological factors which would support the argument that learning a second language should be started as early as possible if the learners wish to become bilingual. At this early age pupils have a better opportunity of establishing long-term memory patterns and of developing a pronunciation which, owing to the plasticity of young children's neuro-muscular structure, is perfect in the majority of cases. Psychologically, almost all young children are highly motivated towards learning a second language, if this language is connected with a world in which the children can satisfy their immediate needs.

Dr. Clare Burstall (1974) in her evaluation of the teaching of French in the primary school, where courses were started at the age of eight and French was taught for one lesson per day, concludes that introducing French in the primary school does not bring overwhelming advantages over starting French in the secondary school at the age of 11 +. However great care should be taken in equating the French project with the Bilingual Education Project. There are many differences, e.g., in the starting age, the time devoted to second-language sessions, the proficiency of teachers in the target language. The greatest differences are, perhaps, to be found in the overall philosophy and methodology of the two projects. In the Bilingual Education Project the second language is not 'taught' in the traditional sense of the word, and goes beyond even highly modern and progressive language approaches where all available aids, audio and visual, are fully utilised, but where the main target still tends to be the language rather than the pupil's education. A single lesson per day at primary school level rather than regular half-day second-language sessions makes it very difficult for most pupils, and teachers, to see the second or foreign language as a tool. They will tend to make the language the primary target of the learning procedure.

(16) As the majority of infant and junior-school teachers are not fully-trained second-language teachers, especially in the type of methodology outlined here, it is vital that all teachers receive at least *some* basic instruction in how to teach in a bilingual education programme before the project is started. This type of second-language education, where the children's overall development is just as important as their acquiring a second language and where both factors are closely interwoven, requires the teacher to gain an increased insight into the ways children learn and develop, and to apply this greater insight and competence when the second language is fused into an enhanced general education. It can be stated categorically that the fewer sound ideas a teacher has about educating children in general, the fewer opportunities he will give his children to develop their second language.

Infant teachers, for instance, will have to know why, when and how children develop concepts and skills, so that the correct sequence of different types of activity can be introduced at the appropriate stage in a child's general development. They will have to know the best ways of presenting and interchanging activities. They will have to know how best to involve children in activities to satisfy developmental needs. They will have to know the total range of concepts and skills which can be developed in different types of activity. Junior-school teachers must know about project work dealing with a variety of topics, and how to introduce the extra-curricular and social aspects of the children's world into the classroom. In fact, the extra-curricular and social aspects of the children's world are already being developed to an increasing extent in the infant school. These are merely a few examples of what teachers must be aware of before the fusion of the second language into activity and other types of work can be effectively accomplished.

To this knowledge about general education must be added knowledge of second-language development and how these two factors are interwoven. Teachers should receive information about level 1 and level 2 communication, language grading, language manipulation, social interactions and the settings in which they occur, preliminary language practice, the phasing of activities in relation to second-language acquisition, the interaction between first and second-language sessions, the satisfaction of immediate needs and all the other items described briefly in the previous pages.

It is clear that such an in-service training cannot be accomplished in a few hours. Furthermore, if the teachers are not fully competent in the second language, further in-service training would be required in language tuition. Each authority will have to decide how much in-service training their teachers must receive before they are required to commence teaching in a bilingual education programme.

Once the programme is under way, the officers who conducted the initial in-service training, must act as field officers, paying regular and frequent visits to the schools participating in the programme. Teachers require a great deal of help and guidance before they can tackle their difficult teaching tasks with confidence and competence.

(17) Before a bilingual education programme is introduced in primary schools, the parents of the children who might take part in such a project, should be fully informed and consulted about the educational and linguistic issues concerned. Most important of all,

their consent and especially their co-operation should be sought. Without such co-operation from parents a bilingual education programme is not likely to succeed. Although in many countries where two languages are spoken, the concept of bilingualism is often a sensitive issue, a large number of parents are nevertheless initially apathetic and raise no objections to their children's participating in the programme. Experience has shown, however, that once the programme is under way and children return home day after day full of enthusiasm about what they have learnt in relation to skills and knowledge as well as language, many parents begin to realise that their children are not merely learning a second language, but that this very process enhances the general education of their children. Indifference soon changes into co-operation, with some monolingual parents even attending language courses to keep up with their children.

On the other hand, if a bilingual education programme is suddenly introduced in a primary school without initial consultation with parents, indifference can quickly develop into hostility against such a scheme. If a school persists with the programme, this hostility is transmitted to the children and it will be impossible to make such a scheme worth while. It might be possible to teach and learn to a greater or lesser extent almost every subject found in the curriculum of a school against the wishes of the pupils, but it is extremely difficult, if not impossible, to create a classroom situation in which a second language can be learnt effectively to bilingual standards without the co-operation of both pupils and parents. Learning a language is not merely the acquisition of knowledge, but also the development of a whole range of linguistic and non-linguistic skills, all of which contribute to the development of communicative competence.

PHASE ONE: PILOT EXPERIMENT IN THE INFANT SCHOOL

When the Schools Council Project on Bilingual Education in the Primary School was initiated in 1968 the Director and his assistant were given approximately one term to prepare materials, grade the second language for infant-school purposes, locate schools prepared to participate, obtain permission from the local authorities concerned, contact headteachers and staff, organise their working offices and prepare teachers for the scheme.

This was obviously too short a time to complete all these tasks satisfactorily. It was fortunate that the Director had been the headmaster of a Welsh-medium school where originally monoglot

English-speaking children developed into bilingual English-Welsh speakers. The Director thus brought with him a vast range of experience concerning the fusion of the second language into the activity work found in infant schools (to which the original Schools Council pilot experiment was confined).

No separate attempt was made to ascertain the interaction processes of children (item 7) and the linguistic items used by them in these processes (item 12), because of the insufficient amount of time available. The Project staff had to rely on their experience for these factors. They also made the assumption that the type of work already being done in the infant schools selected for the Project would prove to fit in with a bilingual education programme, which requires the general development of infants to take place within activity work into which the second language can be fused. However, even as late as six months after the Project had entered the schools, when I was asked to act as an independent evaluator, I discovered that there were still some teachers, though only a few, who had not at this stage understood or taken up the British post-war infant-school approach of structured and phased activity work. It has already been stated that the teacher must understand the factors underlying a structured activity approach before she can begin to learn how to introduce a second language at infant-school level.

Most of the teachers seen, however, were exceedingly good infant teachers but since many of them had little or no knowledge of how to introduce a second language when the Project started, it would have been better for them to have had a series of preliminary in-service training courses providing some information concerning second-language learning processes in relation to general infant work. Owing to the shortage of time, however, it was possible only to hold a single teachers' conference lasting one afternoon at the commencement of the scheme. This would seem to fall far short of what is required for teachers to start their work with confidence.

Instead it was decided to pay regular visits to schools to demonstrate teaching techniques and transmit information. Since there were at this stage some twenty-five schools in the Project, no teacher could be seen more than once a month. At the same time the Project staff were also concerned with the on-going process of producing materials. This must have placed a considerable strain on Project staff, whilst at the same time some teachers were bound to feel uncertain and lacking in confidence at a crucial point in the life of the Project. It is to the credit of both Project staff and teachers that they managed to overcome these initial difficulties and make a success of the Project in the infant school.

Almost all the teachers seen felt most enthusiastic about the scheme, but some of them admitted that initially they had lacked the required confidence and insight into the teaching and learning principles underlying the scheme. A well-organised in-service training programme at the beginning could so easily have prevented some of the difficulties encountered.

Some teachers expected an immediate active linguistic participation by the children. Preliminary experiments showed that some four- and five-year-olds spend weeks trying to become accustomed to the new language, although the activities, to which this language is attached, are wholly pleasurable to them. The child's mind quite rightly, is focused on the activity, and the role of language in relation to this activity depends firstly on the speed with which each individual child is able to acquire, retain and associate the meaning of the second-language sound-chains he hears, and secondly on how much the child wishes to satisfy his immediate needs to execute the activity satisfactorily through the medium of the second language. Acquisition, retention and association may take some time; the child will tend not to speak second-language phrases or sentences unless the activity requires it. Some teachers became disheartened at the beginning because certain children would not switch immediately to making active use of the language (i.e. level 2 communication). If the teachers had been aware, from the beginning, of the learner's progression through level 1 to level 2 communication in relation to particular activities, they might have been saved that agonizing loss of confidence and the children's progress have consequently been speeded up.

Ideally, the activities should have been graded to allow children initially to play their way through either class or group games in which their minds were focused on language and game in order to complete as individuals a particular aspect of the game from the point of view of both understanding and using language. Many of the successful teachers, for example, played a preliminary 'command and execute' language game to help children learn patterns and vocabulary which could be made use of later on in a more complex and continuous activity.

The teacher would have available a whole range of objects: boxes, pencils, clay, dolls, paper, blackboard, water, paintbrushes, etc., and a whole variety of toys. Initially she would give a command, e.g., the Welsh equivalent of 'Put the paintbrush in the water!' or 'Put the pencil in the box!' and execute the activity herself. At times she would give the children the mother-tongue equivalent, especially if some children still looked puzzled of if a child asked for the meaning. At other times some children would guess at the meaning without being asked. If the meaning was incorrect, she would give the correct meaning. She would then ask individual children to carry out the various commands, leading eventually to the children themselves giving the commands. Usually this was followed by making the child who was carrying out the command, describe his action in the first person after this had been learnt in the same way. Question forms were tackled similarly in the same or different games. All these preliminary activities were always carried out in a spirit of excitement, laced with a good deal of laughter especially if, through permutation of language, some odd commands were made, e.g., 'Put the baby (doll) in the shoe!' This level 1 communication activity was then followed by a normal infant-school activity, e.g., painting or playing with clay, to develop physical skills and a sense of design and proportion. The children would now be able to make use of the language learnt during the preliminary language game both to execute the activity and to consolidate the language further. Now, however, language had been raised to level 2; it had become a tool.

The more successful teachers were able to introduce all new patterns and vocabulary through these initial games, some of which were 'matching games' such as 'Lotto,' others more active games in the hall or the playground, e.g., dancing, street games or physical education. Everything learnt at level 1 was always followed by an activity where children could make use of their new language as a vehicle of communication at level 2. If all teachers had understood this progression within activities, and how to implement such a progression, the Project could have been even more successful at the infant school during the initial years.

In my internal report of 1970 I mention that at first some of the teachers observed did not distinguish between 'aids' and 'equipment' or 'resource materials' used for language teaching, mainly because they considered language even at this early stage to be predominantly a verbal activity. The idea that in a communicative event language is only a part and not the whole had either not been understood or not transmitted during the visits made by Project staff. It was significant during my own visits that many teachers demonstrated the work done so far by giving almost

22

formal oral lessons, reminiscent of secondary-school language teaching, where spoken responses were elicited by verbal stimuli only, with or without visual aids. In only a few schools was a deliberate attempt made to show how the children were able in play activities to make use of language (at level 2) learnt during previous preliminary language-learning activities and games (at level 1).

It was also noticed that in some instances 'equipment' or 'resource materials' intended for activity work at level 2 was instead used solely as a 'visual aid', which the children could look at and which was used for learning how to speak questions and answers at level 1, but which was not played with in a Welsh context where language could develop into a tool. Examples of this were animals and equipment relating to a farm, a garage, and in one isolated instance a tea service which was used only by the teacher as an aid but which was out of bounds for the pupils.

By March 1970 it was possible to detect three main patterns in the linguistic development of the children. Each individual school tended in the main to reflect one of these patterns though there were, of course, individual children in every school who followed the other patterns.

Group 1
In the first group of schools there were children who had developed a remarkable degree of communicative competence. The levels reached were so high that personal doubts arose as to whether their exceptionally good second-language development had been accomplished at the expense of their growth in other areas of the school curriculum. I had to accept teachers' and headteachers' assurances that their children's development had, if anything improved. At this stage the Schools Council had not appointed a Senior Research Officer responsible for ascertaining the children's progress in English and Arithmetic as compared with that of children not participating in the Project. Now that the results of these comparative tests are available, the initial doubts about the children's total development can be dispelled, since the Project work had no detrimental effect on the children's general development in other subjects.

The high linguistic competence of these children was exhibited mainly during activity work when children were left to themselves. They attempted, and on most occasions, managed to communicate throughout in Welsh in order to execute their activities. It was also found that many of the infants corrected each other or offered the occasional word to a friend who could not complete his sentence or did not know the meaning of a word.

What impressed most was the children's ability to utilise known speech patterns by substituting relevant vocabulary to satisfy their needs. It has already been stated that the skill of permutating vocabulary in known speech patterns is the most important *linguistic* skill to be acquired during the language-learning process. The teachers were aware of this and made certain that their children received ample preliminary level 1 work in language games related to subsequent activities. Some even introduced short bursts of pure language work which could be described as drill work. Yet the atmosphere remained happy with the children continuing to practise these speech patterns without prompting in their play corners after the drill work had ceased. All the preliminary language work, either in games or in drills, reflected the type of short-cuts the young bilingual child takes when strengthening his second language in relation to his preferred language. The work consisted either of imitation (with meaning), interpretation or substitution activities. When the teacher had placed some stress on intonation patterns, some of the children once again went voluntarily to their corners to continue their practice whilst playing with a toy. Whenever they had run out of sentences some would continue their intonation practice by speaking some Welsh-sounding gibberish. All these voluntary and obviously pleasurable acts confirm the view that the actual communicative events within an activity do not in themselves afford the learner sufficient opportunity to reach communicative competence, but that the learner, like his bilingual counterpart, will try to find short-cuts where he can focus his mind in a more concentrated manner on language itself so as to develop all the more rapidly a level of communicative competence in order to cope with his environment.

Yet these teachers were fully aware that this preliminary language work does not in itself produce communicative competence but that such competence can only develop in the general activities relating to the real world, where language can become a tool and where children will eventually reach a stage where they are no longer aware of the second language when they make use of it. One often hears that the ideal stage to be reached is to 'think in the language'. Do we not really mean by 'thinking in the language' that we are no longer 'thinking about the language' when we are making use of it?

Group 2

In the second group of schools, which were in the majority, most children, though they had dealt diligently with the preliminary language work, were not always successful in adapting the basic language which they had learnt, once free activity commenced. Further analysis showed that these children had in fact learnt a range of set sentences but had not realised that these sentences belonged to pattern groups, the elements of which could be interchanged.

Faced with a classroom procedure where the teacher gave a known type of spoken stimulus, the children would readily respond with the sentences learnt previously. They had through constant repetition learnt to respond to given situations. As soon as the spoken stimulus was changed to express an unfamiliar concept, the responses tended to cease. It was, therefore, difficult for those children to make a great deal of use of the sentences in subsequent activity work, which on most occasions is not predictable in detail.

Nevertheless, this group had managed to learn a new set of sentences for their play activities, and in order to show that they were in fact using Welsh during these activities, they adjusted their activities to make the language material learnt relevant. This was in complete contrast to the first group of children who adjusted their language to cope with the activities.

Within this group there were also schools who had placed great stress on level 2 activity work but had neglected the preliminary language work relating to specific activities. These schools in many ways reflected in their procedures what is called an immediate 'language bath', and it became clear very soon that most children had less confidence and less ability in the manipulation of language than the other children within this group, especially if compared with the first group who had struck a proper balance between correct preliminary language work and subsequent related activities, all of which were executed in the second language. The amount of activity work done by the first group and the amount of language used within those activities, which were in fact true language-bath situations, was greater than that found in the schools who assumed it was possible to reach communicative competence by throwing children into a 'sea of language', graded or not, without giving children an opportunity to take necessary practice steps at level 1 in order to reach level 2 communication.

Group 3
The third group of children consisted of a small minority of children who were taught by unimaginative teachers who made preliminary language work unpleasant by taking all the elements of

play out of it and by introducing too much language material at a time. In many ways these teachers thought more of the language than the children. Subsequent activity work, if any, was often unrelated to the preliminary work and hence could not be tackled by the children in terms of the second language. The two teachers in this category were in fact teachers not trained in infant work, and this could have had a bearing on their general approach.

By 1970 the phasing of concepts (item 9) between first- and second-language sessions had not been developed to any degree. Nor had the progression of activities in relation to language and the general development of children over the three years at the infant school been formulated or investigated. Nevertheless, it seemed clear at that time that it would be possible for the second group of schools to develop the type of teaching and learning found in the first group where children had developed a high degree of communicative competence. It was for this reason that it was eventually decided to extend the Project into the junior school.

PHASE TWO: INFANT AND JUNIOR SCHOOLS

When the decision to extend the Project into the junior school had been confirmed, some of the children were already due to move into the junior school. Once again the Project staff had very little time to prepare the necessary language and resource materials. There was also an additional factor which had to be taken into account. Whilst activity work was the norm in the infant school, many junior schools used more formal approaches in the education of the children. Although requests were made by the Project team to extend activity work into the junior school, it was considered important to develop at the same time a series of areas which could be tackled by both teachers and pupils through normal 'project work'. Areas such as 'Water', 'The Town', 'The Harbour' were developed by the team or school, in the hope that the type of activity work done in the infant school could be continued in the junior school, though in a more sophisticated form pitched at the maturation level of the children. It is true to say, however, that almost a whole year was lost before the Project team was able to establish a pattern into which to place a bilingual education programme in junior schools.

In the meantime the work in the infant schools continued with new annual intakes of children. Before returning to the junior schools it would be appropriate to conclude the assessment of the infant schools up to 1975.

A large number of schools with children falling within the second category of proficiency were able to adjust to more efficient procedures. Exchanges of experience with other teachers and regular visits made by the now enlarged Project team brought about the pooling of successfully used activities, so that more and more children were able to communicate at level 2. This is a most encouraging development but the pleasure of success should be tempered by the fact that during discussions with teachers it was clear that many of them had not grasped the point concerning a) the learners' development through level 1 and level 2 communication for any topic or activity area and b) the progression and phasing of activities. These teachers had succeeded, however, because they had closely followed the procedures used by the initially successful teachers, which had later been demonstrated in their schools by Project team members.

It could be argued that this is sufficient for a proper development of new approaches in the education of children, but such a course brings with it disadvantages. My 1970 report recommended that the Project should examine the concept areas and their related infant-school activities which would have to be fused into the bilingual education programme to ensure the sound concept development of children over the years. This work was eventually done and has appeared in the teachers' book (Schools Council, 1975). During the lifetime of the Project it was noted however, that many of the activities found in any one year of the infant school were repeated in subsequent years, albeit by different teachers, and hence in a slightly modified form. Since the type of language attached to these activities remained largely the same, linguistic progress tended to be slowed down. It is interesting to note that the research report by Dr. E. Price states (see p.91) 'In oral expression as well as in levels of comprehension it appears that roughly the same level of attainment is reached whether the Project is implemented for two or three years in the infant schools. One is prompted to wonder why, if this level of attainment can be reached in two years, a third year does not extend the pupils still further.' A more or less haphazard selection of activities without due regard to progression and phrasing could be responsible for this otherwise surprising finding.

Item 17 of this report deals with the need to obtain parents' consent and co-operation through prior consultations and discussions. Whilst this procedure was followed in many instances, there were cases where this was omitted or not properly followed through. There was a great deal of evidence that quite a few teachers had to convince individual parents of the effectiveness and purpose of the scheme *after* the introduction of the Project in their schools. This should not have been the teachers' responsibility and placed an unreasonable burden on them. In one instance lack of public relations work caused a major upset which was taken up by the media, forcing the local education authority to revert to their pre-Project plan of having a series of Welsh lessons during the school week. It should be added, however, that after further consultations, parents themselves eventually voted for a return to the Schools Council procedure of daily Welsh sessions.

In an age when participation in decision-making about our future and that of our children is becoming more crucial if we wish to develop our democratic way of life, no parent should be, and in fact can be, forced to make his or her child take part in a project which for him or her touches upon extremely sensitive language issues, no matter how much the organisers desire a uniform and, therefore, simpler educational pattern. This view is fully supported by the Gittins Report (1967), on which the Schools Council Project is based, with regard to the establishment of bilingual schools. What was encouraging about this Project was that, of the small number of originally hostile parents (usually made so as a result of lack of information and knowledge about the Project), many eventually changed their attitudes once they realised that the children were not learning Welsh at the expense of anything else and that in many instances the general education of children had improved because of the existence of the Project.

It had originally been assumed that the more crucial concept areas affecting children's development should be excluded from the Welsh sessions in the infant school. It became clear in the early 1970s that some of these concepts, especially those relating to numeracy, were being consolidated during the Welsh sessions to the benefit of children. What in fact was developing were the first natural steps towards the 'teaching' of arithmetic through the medium of Welsh, an activity which the children thoroughly enjoyed and which, of course, was an additional contact with arithmetic. Furthermore, many teachers began to attach bilingual instead of English monolingual name cards to all parts of the classroom, so that before long the Welsh printed word became an additional tool in the children's reading repertoire. None of these activities has had any detrimental effects whatsoever on the children's development in English or Arithmetic, as the research report has shown, but they have strengthened the children's command of Welsh more than the traditional approach, where Welsh as a subject is an end in itself. Taking all these factors into account, and noting all the lessons learnt, I have pleasure in reporting that both linguistically and educationally the Project has been a success in many of the infant schools.

Everyone concerned in the organisation of the Project was aware that the extension of the work into the junior school would be a far more difficult task than the original introduction in the infant schools. Most of the junior-school teachers had had experience in the teaching of Welsh, but mainly in the context of one short lesson per day given to children who were in most instances beginning to learn Welsh for the first time in the junior schools. It has already been stated that under more formal conditions in the context of daily Welsh lessons, both teachers and pupils will tend to make the language the prime focus of the learning procedure, unless schools are supplied with, or are prepared to make, a series of resource materials relating to various aspects of human knowledge and behaviour. These resource materials, not to be confused with language materials, would enable pupils to adjust their focus of attention away from language onto other fields of interest, so that language could be made use of as a tool, as described earlier in this report in the analysis of communication levels 1 and 2.

This view of language development had not, however, penetrated deeply in the junior schools, and in many instances language teaching resembled the type of work which still takes place in many of our secondary schools, even with modern teaching aids. Teachers, pupils and parents had felt for years that the amount of time and effort spent was not really worth while. It was against this general background that the Schools Council Project entered the junior school. Some teachers had to be persuaded that the Project was feasible and not merely an extension of the single-lesson format which had proved so disappointing. Most of them needed in-service training to cope with activity and 'project' work in relation to second-language development. Unfortunately the timing of the decision to extend the Project into the junior school left little time for this adjustment to be made satisfactorily. It should also be stated that, although the Project team had a) clearly defined their objectives concerning bilingual education, b) developed a whole range of activities and projects, and c) graded patterns and vocabulary, the clear and simple differences between communication levels 1 and 2, between 'learning and using' and 'making use of' language, between satisfying linguistic needs and satisfying immediate needs other than those of language, had not been clearly defined within an overall methodology which could have been given to teachers. Yet these factors were all present in the observed demonstrations given by Project staff when in schools. It is felt that a clear and simple explanation of a methodological framework showing how any activity or series of activities could be used to lead children through communication level 1 to level 2 in any area of experience would have made the teachers' task less difficult. Instead teachers themselves had to abstract these factors from the demonstrations for later application with their own activities. It should not be surprising that a good proportion of them did not become clearly aware of the issues involved and instead merely imitated the items seen in the demonstrations. This is not to say, of course, that many teachers did not continue admirably with the work already started in the infant school. At this stage in the report it might be appropriate to deal with the more difficult aspects of the Project first, before dealing with the real successes in the junior school.

Some of the teachers observed during that part of the day when subjects such as 'Arts and Crafts' were dealt with through the medium of English were able to motivate children to a high degree. As soon as the language was changed, a more 'academic' approach became noticeable and the eagerness and enjoyment seen previously tended to disappear. Whilst in one respect it might be possible to equate this work with level 1 work, because the pupils' minds are focused on language, these teachers had not yet learnt to make the work a pleasurable and relevant exercise. In the main the work tended to be too abstract. It would have been better if the teachers had fused what to the observer was preliminary work into an interesting situational context, or had used dialogues instead of narratives, or had learnt to use particular types of drill work which children enjoy. After this work the observer expected the children to make use of the language they had learnt in relevant subsequent activities. Often he had to wait in vain because the children did not leave their desks but instead continued with writing work. At other times the children were directed towards different activities which, however, had little bearing on the language learnt previously.

The 'Arts and Crafts' lesson mentioned above could in fact easily have been used for both level 1 *and* level 2 work in Welsh. For instance, the teacher could teach the class the patterns and vocabulary needed in learning how to make a collage. During this level 1 process the children would be learning to understand and speak the necessary sentences, together with the permutation of the vocabulary within these sentences, whilst the teacher would at all times attach this language to the various materials, drawings and demonstrated skills which the children had yet to handle and master. This level 1 work, which need not take more than ten or fifteen minutes at a time, could then be followed immediately by the children beginning to learn to make their own collages through the medium of Welsh. In other words, they would be making use of Welsh in order to satisfy something which is not linguistic. That is level 2 communication, and should be the aim of a bilingual education programme for any activity, topic, area of knowledge or range of skills. Language items not properly learnt or not yet made automatic by a particular child could be strengthened during the making of the collage or, if many pupils showed the same weak linguistic point, could be reinforced during subsequent level 1 work relating to a different activity. On the other hand, there would be no harm in interrupting the collage-making for a quick return to level 1 language work but followed again immediately by level 2 collage work.

It should be obvious that there are a large number of areas in the school curriculum which lend themselves to this approach; eventually, however, all 'subjects' and not merely the more practical ones, can be taught through the medium of the second language.

Some of the junior-school teachers experienced the same difficulties as those experienced initially by infant-school teachers. Some tended to restrict language to level 1 only, whilst others had difficulties in developing level 1 work or making it relevant and interesting. Others introduced level 2 work unrelated to level 1 work, whilst a further group omitted level 1 work altogether with disastrous consequences at level 2.

It was also noted that some teachers became inhibited during level 2 work and did not reflect the zest and spirit exhibited during equivalent English-medium work. As it is difficult for any teacher to remember the particular language, behaviour and ideas which have motivated children to a high degree at various points during lessons already given, and hence difficult to transfer these items to Welsh level 2 sessions, it was suggested that teachers could be helped if they, together with Project members, made an interaction analysis of those English-medium lessons they knew were enjoyed by the children. Although this suggestion was made in 1972 it was only applied in two schools in 1974 in one trial run. The teachers concerned began to enjoy the analysis and one Project officer reported that a teacher felt it had given her new insights into her own teaching. Although the teacher requested to continue the work, it was considered unwise to concentrate Project staff on a few schools, when so many other teachers also required help, especially as the life of the Project was coming to an end and no extension had at that stage been granted. It would have been possible, however, to have shown teachers how to make this analysis themselves with the aid of a tape recorder.

It should also be mentioned that some teachers found it difficult to implement the newly prepared projects on the various topics. Some either ignored them or spent too much time on individual projects. There was also a suspicion that in some schools the time devoted to Welsh sessions fell short of that suggested by the School Council.

Despite all these difficulties there are a good number of junior schools in all parts of Wales where children are reaching a level of communicative competence in Welsh far higher than could have been expected from the first experimental cohort passing through the primary school. It has been a pleasure to visit these schools, where children even at the early age of eight or nine are beginning to reach an acceptable level of bilingualism in a wide range of spheres of their young lives. The children feel, and look, happy and are brought into contact with all types of knowledge, developing skills and behaviour patterns leading to a fully integrated education, without which the learning of a second language cannot be accomplished. Although all the teachers involved are aware of the children's natural language progression in the second language through levels 1 and 2, each teacher tackles his task according to his own personality and skills. Some allow their children to reach communicative competence mainly through project work in which a whole range of resource materials are made and used by themselves and the children, others focus more on a 'subject-biased' junior school approach, leading children gently in their second language through physical education, dancing, art, gardening, play-acting, nature study, biology, local history and geography and a host of other areas.

In one school I spent an enlightening afternoon where I could not help but learn from the children and the teacher all about the geology of the area, especially as I was surrounded by a vast number of rocks, huge home-made wall charts, tools, maps and cross-sectional diagrams of the earth beneath me. The children were full of language, drawn out of them by the excitement of the event, each new discovery about a rock, brought in by a child and carefully split in the classroom, eliciting requests for new words and phrases. When a sufficient number of new words and phases had been given, the children gladly huddled around the teacher for a quick consolidation practice of these language items, in the knowledge that this extended language would help them to communicate any further discoveries made immediately afterwards to their teacher and other members of the class. Here language was a real tool and not something to be learnt for its own sake.

All these teachers informed me that they laid great stress on preliminary language work within related activities which could be used as springboards for more sophisticated work, as described above. Furthermore, they reported that the children enjoyed these preliminary activities not only because they were interesting in themselves but also because they were always followed by further exciting work. Once more it has to be said that these children were making use of their second language because they were able to satisfy their immediate needs in relation to something which was not language.

Although some schools suffered from shortages of suitably qualified bilingual teachers, or were not always given bilingual replacements when a Project teacher left, this need not have been in every case an insuperable problem since not all teachers in a school need to be bilingual; only half the children's day is devoted to 'Welsh' sessions, so that a properly planned staffing arrangement could satisfy the essential needs of 'bilingual education' under such less than ideal conditions. The use of specialist teachers of Welsh (originally intended for single-lesson procedures) was not considered fully satisfactory by the Project. Yet observations made in schools where such an arrangement was properly implemented, confirm that such a procedure is more than acceptable, and that the results obtained were far higher in quality than those obtained in schools where a fully bilingual staff had not properly understood the requirements of the second-language learner. The specialist teacher, after having made himself acquainted with all the various aspects of the school's bilingual education programme in the various classes, was able to go from class to class and help children practise their level 1 work within related activities.

For example, the specialist could be dealing with various varieties of birds and their habitats. After he has left for another class, the children could continue with their normal class teacher in activities where one group makes cardboard nesting boxes for the birds previously dealt with, others might work in the 'hobby' corner where they arrange, classify and describe birds' feathers they have collected themselves, whilst a third group could be busily involved studying the behaviour of a budgerigar belonging to one of the pupils, followed by cleaning out the birds' cage and seeing to its feeding needs. During all these activities the class teacher, who knows what language has been dealt with by the specialist, moves from one group to the other encouraging children to consolidate and make use of the second language. This generalised example is based on observations made in schools and shows that the important business of the children's learning about the world is not being neglected.

It should be clear that once teachers have caught on to the basic principles of a bilingual education programme, the children will encounter many facets of the world which everyone feels should be taught in schools but which for various reasons are omitted in the normal routine of many primary schools.

A heartening development during the life of the Project was the introduction of a week's visit to a local authority holiday centre located on the beautiful shores of Lake Bala. In the course of their week's stay in the company of their teachers, children continued with daily learning sessions related to all the aspects of the centre, but now the language used throughout the rest of the day was Welsh. Extra-curricular and social aspects of the children's world could be fully utilised. Meals in the dining-room, games, sports, swimming, boating, community singing, inter-school and individual competitions in art, essay-writing, the production of project materials, and all the other activities possible in such a centre, were conducted through the medium of the second language. The children had the time of their lives, but the important point to remember is that they were able to satisfy their immediate non-linguistic needs whilst they were making use of the second language. It would be desirable if such a scheme could be extended by giving children an opportunity to spend part of their school holidays with Welsh-speaking families in the more Welsh-speaking areas of the Principality.

Many of the successful schools included role-playing in their Welsh sessions, especially at the infant level. It would have been encouraging if more of this work had been done in the junior school. Although the successful schools had regular role-playing, the other schools usually confined themselves to preparing performances for Christmas, St. David's Day and Parents' Day. It was noted, however, that this role-playing normally took the form of 'role-taking' in set playlets, an activity which refers mainly to level 1 communication. This work should be extended to 'role-making' through a series of graded steps. It is in 'role-making' performances that level 2 communication and communicative competence can flourish. 'Role-making' was observed in some schools where children performed, often spontaneously, their own little plays, involving, for example, the Daleks from the TV Dr Who programmes, or a version of 'Robin Hood' created on the spot in the setting of a Welsh valley.

It has already been mentioned that in the infant school, bilingual name-cards were found in different parts of the classroom. The use of the Welsh printed word was gradually extended into story books, from words to sentences which children began to associate with all the language items they could already understand and speak. Even before children left the infant school they began to read and write the Welsh they could speak, so that in the junior school reading and writing work in Welsh became a natural development in the children's growth in the second language. The Project team produced a large number of first-rate 'talking' (non-printed word) books and story-books together with a range of other materials in which the printed word occurred. All this reinforced the children's progress in understanding, speaking, reading and writing the second language.

The real worth of such a bilingual education programme is ultimately reflected in the influence it has had on parents and pupils. Some children from the more successful primary schools and belonging to the first cohort leaving the junior school in 1975 have opted to enter Welsh-medium secondary schools. If it is remembered that this cohort suffered all the difficulties and short-comings in the initial stages of the life of the Project, this development is astounding. Some dozen or so children from one school in an English-speaking area with English-speaking parents entered a Welsh-medium secondary school last year. Whilst I understand that three of these children were not able to cope in this school and transferred to an English-medium secondary school (where, it is hoped, a secondary-school bilingual education programme might eventually be introduced), such progress is nonetheless astonishing and exceeds anything that could reasonably have been expected at the beginning of the Project.

Nevertheless it should be remembered that these children came from the more successful schools and a great deal of work has yet to be done in the remaining schools to help teachers and pupils. When the first Director left to return to his own school towards the end of the Project, the work was taken over by the National Language Unit of Wales. The Schools Council wisely decided that the Project should be continued after 1975 and that an after-care service should be made available. Two field officers were appointed to carry on with this work until 1977. I should like to take this opportunity to make the strongest recommendation possible for a continuation and a strengthening of such an after-care service beyond 1977. This report should make it clear that, although there have been many breakthroughs in a large number of schools, there are still too many areas where help and clarification are needed, especially now that there are many schools not yet under the care of the Project who wish to introduce a bilingual education programme, and are in fact doing so completely on their own.

One thing that has become clear is that sheer enthusiasm is not enough to make bilingual education what it should be. Teachers require also the knowledge and the practical expertise to help them sustain such a programme. Moreover it would seem imperative that Colleges of Education and University Departments of Education should train our future primary-school Welsh-speaking teachers more intensively in the various aspects of a bilingual education programme. Only then can we hope for some guarantee that such a development will continue in our primary schools. Should we fail to look ahead in our educational decision-making there is the danger of our reverting to where we were before the Project was started in 1968, and this would nullify all the recommendations made in the Gittins Report concerning bilingual education.

Finally, I should like to thank both Project directors, Mr G. E. Richards and Mr E. Evans, and the various field officers who so readily put up with my questioning and probing and who allowed me to accompany them to the schools. I should also like to thank the many headteachers and staff for the friendly reception and generous hospitality given to me at all times during visits made with field officers or on my own.

For references see page 182

Bilingual Education Programmes in Wales and Canada

J. CUMMINS AND F. GENESEE

THERE ARE many parallels between Wales and Canada in terms of the role of bilingualism in education. In both countries, a minority language group is attempting to resist assimilation and maintain its language and culture in the face of the increasing influence of the majority language. Over the past fifteen years, members of the majority language group in both countries have become increasingly interested in learning the minority language. This latter trend, together with wide-spread dissatisfaction with traditional methods of second language teaching, has given rise to several innovative bilingual education programmes designed to promote proficiency in a second language at no cost to students' first language proficiency or to overall academic achievement.

In this paper we shall compare the pedagogical assumptions underlying these innovative bilingual programmes as well as research findings on their effects. Experiences in each country have influenced the development of bilingual education in the other, and our purpose is to contribute to this mutually beneficial process of cross-fertilization.

In Canada, the main provision for teaching French to English-speaking children remains the traditional French-as-a-second-language (FSL) programme in which French is taught as a subject for between 20 and 40 minutes per day. However, immersion programmes which use French as a medium of instruction for all or part of the school day have increased rapidly across Canada during the past ten years. It is estimated that there are currently at least 50,000 students in various types of French immersion programmes (Cummins and Lapkin, in preparation).

A range of starting grades is found in immersion programmes; so-called 'early' immersion programmes usually start in kindergarten, while the most common starting grade for 'late' immersion programmes is grade 7. Also, in recent years, several school boards have introduced 'intermediate' immersion programmes starting in grades 4 and 5. Within all these options, the time allotted to instruction in French varies considerably but is usually between 50 and 100 per cent of the school day.

In the provinces of Ontario, Manitoba and New Brunswick minority francophone students usually attend separate schools in which a major part of the curriculum (50-80%) is taught through French. The cultural component in these curricula is considered extremely important for the maintenance of French, and anglophone students are not encouraged to attend these schools. In Manitoba, for example, francophone organizations have been active in supporting the expansion of immersion programmes for anglophone students, partly because they were concerned that the increasing enrolment of anglophone students in francophone schools would dilute the cultural and linguistic emphasis of their programme. In other provinces outside Quebec where the concentration of minority francophones is less, integration of anglophone and francophone students in the same bilingual schools is more common.

Four main types of provision for the acquisition of Welsh by children whose first language is English can be distinguished: (1) traditional programmes of Welsh-as-a-second-language (WSL) in which Welsh is taught for approximately half an hour per day; (2) Welsh medium schools in comparatively anglicized areas—the so-called 'Ysgolion Cymraeg'; (3) Welsh medium schools in areas where Welsh is the principal language of the local community; (4) the recent Schools Council Bilingual Project approach in which Welsh is used as the medium of instruction for part of the school day.

Each of these types of provision will be considered in turn and the parallels between similar programmes in Welsh and Canadian contexts will be examined.

TRADITIONAL SECOND LANGUAGE PROGRAMMES

The ineffectiveness of the traditional policy of exposing anglophone children to half an hour a day of Welsh in the junior school is commented on by Evans:

> 'To state the matter bluntly, this policy, at least until quite recently, has been a disastrous failure. Even the minority Welsh speaking elements in these second language schools frequently failed to retain their natural bilingualism and lapsed into becoming monoglot English speakers.' (1976, p. 54-55)

The situation has improved in recent years as a result of the development of WSL materials and courses by the National Language Unit. However, despite these advances it is unlikely that children in these programmes will make much progress towards bilingualism because of the inherent limitations of this approach. In Canada, an increasing number of educators and parents also acknowledge the limitations of French-as-a-second-language alone and consequently many FSL programmes in the elementry school now feed into intermediate or late immersion programmes (Genesee, Polich and Stanley, 1977; Genesee, 1981). However, only a handful of schools in Wales operate programmes similar to late immersion, and, thus, there is virtually no provision for an intensive follow-up to WSL programmes at the secondary school level.

SECOND LANGUAGE IMMERSION PROGRAMMES

Although the Ysgolion Cymraeg were established to serve the needs of small minorities of Welsh-speaking children, they now admit all children whose parents desire them to attend. Indeed, in some schools over 90% of the students come from homes where Welsh is not spoken. There are now over fifty primary and eleven secondary Ysgolion Cymraeg. Welsh is the official language of the school and is used as the sole medium of instruction at the infant level and as the main medium at the junior level. Welsh continues to be used as a major medium for much of the curriculum in secondary school.

The approach in the Ysgolion Cymraeg is clearly similar in many respects to that of early total immersion programmes in Canada (Genesee, 1978). A major difference, however, is that whereas Ysgolion Cymraeg constitute centres for Welsh instruction, immersion programmes generally exist as one stream within an otherwise English school. Immersion centres for anglophone children, where French is the major language of the entire school, are relatively uncommon in Canada. Where such immersion centres have been established there has often been bitter opposition from parents of children in the English stream who have resented the 'loss' of their neighbourhood school.

An extremely large number of evaluations has been carried out on both early and late immersion programmes in Canada. In both types of programme, evaluations have consistently reported that students achieve relatively high levels of French skills at no cost to achievement in English or other academic subjects. Students typically approach native francophone levels in reading and listening skills but not in speaking or writing skills (see Genesee, 1978, for a review). Moreover, it has been found that even students

39

of below average ability (Genesee, 1976), those from low socioeconomic homes (Cziko, 1975) and those with native language difficulties (Bruck, 1978) can benefit from immersion programmes. That is to say, these types of children acquire significantly more proficiency in all aspects of French than similar children in traditional FSL programmes and, at the same time, they suffer no loss in native language development or academic achievement.

Comparisons of students in early immersion programmes and late immersion programmes that provide extensive instruction (80%) for two consecutive years, usually grades 7 and 8, have yielded mixed results. Research in the Montreal area has found that two-year late immersion students achieve the same level of proficiency in all aspects of French as do early immersion students (see Adiv and Morcos, 1979; and Genesee, 1981). In contrast, research carried out in the Ottawa school systems has found that early immersion students score consistently higher than the late immersion students (Morrison, 1979). It is interesting to note that at least one aspect of the early immersion programmes in these two regions that differs noticeably is the amount of follow-up provided in French during the elementary and early secondary school grades. Specifically, the Montreal programme provides approximately 70% in grade 3, 60% in grade 4 and then 40% in grades 6 to 8; the Ottawa programme offers 80% in grades 3, 4 and 5, and 50% in grades 6 to 8. Thus, it would appear from a consideration of this factor alone that the follow-up programme plays an important role in promoting the early immersion students' second language skills. It would also appear from the Montreal results that older students can be effective second language learners possibly as a result of their cognitive maturity.

Unlike the Canadian immersion programmes, the achievement of students in Ysgolion Cymraeg has not been evaluated in any systematic way. However, these schools are generally perceived as having high academic standards, so much so that, at the secondary level, they have sometimes been accused of being elitist or 'disguised grammar schools'. In general, the development of bilingual skills in these schools is regarded as satisfactory, although, according to Evans, 'difficulties occur in promoting the informal and spontaneous use of Welsh in the free play of the children' (1976, p. 55).

BILINGUAL SCHOOLS IN MINORITY LANGUAGE COMMUNITIES

Schools in Welsh-speaking areas have traditionally used Welsh as the exclusive medium of instruction for native Welsh-speaking children at the infant stage (ages 5 to 7) and as the main medium of instruction at the junior stage (ages 7 to 11). However, in some areas there has been a tendency to switch to English by the age of 8 or 9, and most secondary schools have used English as the main or exculsive medium of instruction.

As a result of their increasing awareness of assimilation, the demand among minority francophones for their own French-language schools at both primary and secondary levels has intensified during the past fifteen years. The right of minority francophones to French-language instruction is acknowledged in most provinces, although adminstrative and financial considerations make implementation of this right problematic in settings where the concentration of francophones is low.

There are considerable differences between Wales and Canada in the methods typically used to introduce the second language to English speakers in these bilingual schools. In Wales children from English-speaking homes may attend Welsh-language primary schools either through parental choice or because no English-medium school is available in the area. In some primary schools, children from English-speaking homes are taught partly through Welsh from the start, but usually English is the main initial medium of instruction so that reading is introduced in English. Thus, instruction given to the majority of the class in Welsh is repeated in English for the anglophone children. As the anglophone children's control of Welsh grows through involvement in the mixed language school situation, the use of English as medium of instruction is gradually reduced so that the learning experiences of the children with different linguistic backgrounds become increasingly integrated.

In Canada, French is used as the major medium of instruction for both francophone and anglophone students from the start of the programme, although in the initial grades francophone and anglophone students may be segregated. A large-scale research study carried out in Manitoba has shown that for francophone students, amount of instruction through French was significantly related to French achievement but unrelated to English achievement; in other words, students receiving 80% instruction through French performed as well in English as students receiving 80% instruction through English (Hébert et al., 1976). Similar findings for francophone students are reported in a study conducted in Alberta (Carey and Cummins, 1979).

THE SCHOOLS COUNCIL BILINGUAL PROJECT

Although the time allotted to Welsh in the Schools Council Bilingual Project (SCBP) is probably similar, on the average, to 'extended' French programmes in Canada (usually 70-90 minutes per day) in which one other subject, in addition to French, is taught through the medium of French, the methodology developed in the context of the SCBP is different in many respects from that of other bilingual programmes. The SCBP has its origin in the Gittins Report (Central Advisory Council for Education (Wales), 1967) which recommended the establishment of 'bilingual schools' for anglophone students which would make systematic use of Welsh as a part-time medium of instruction in the infant and junior schools. The Report also suggested that Welsh could be learned effectively if it were used during play activity and as a medium of instruction for 'peripheral' subjects which constitute half of the school day. In 1968 the recommendations of the Gittins Report were implemented in the Schools Council Project on 'Bilingual Education in the Primary Schools in Anglicized Areas'. Sixty schools originally participated in this project and in recent years an increasing number of primary schools in anglicized areas have adopted the SCBP approach to teaching Welsh as a second language.

The teaching methodology of the SCBP has been influenced considerably by the theoretical work of C. J. Dodson (Dodson, 1967; Dodson, Price and Williams, 1968) who argues that effective second language learning will result only if opportunities for meaningful communication are integrated with the teaching of the structure of the language itself. Dodson (1978) proposed a distinction between medium-orientated communication and message-orientated communication which, he claims, ought to be an integral part of every language activity unit in the infant and junior schools. In medium-orientated communication, the child's mind is focused mainly on the language itself, whereas in message-orientated communication the child's aim is to communicate a message which is not about language, so that language is the tool rather than the focus of attention. Dodson (1967, 1978) outlined a cycle of learning activities designed to lead the learner from medium-orientated imitation work towards message-orientated creative use of the second language. In addition to emphasizing the need for a sequential progression from imitation to communicative use of the second language, Dodson also argued that children's first language should be used as a short-cut to meaning, when necessary. At the infant stage in the SCBP schools, the teacher introduces play activities to the children in Welsh as well as in English and attempts to consolidate and extend children's control of Welsh through the use of brief, frequently practised language drills which are disguised as play activities. One example is the 'command and execute' game in which the teacher commands the children to manipulate a series of objects in a variety of ways, e.g., 'Put the paintbrush in the water.' Initially the teacher demonstrates the activity and asks individual children to carry out the commands; afterwards, the children themselves give the commands to one another. In the next stage, the children carry out the commands and describe their actions in the first person. In this way learning of vocabulary and grammatical patterns is disguised by the excitement and fun of the activity. According to Dodson, it is crucial that the drills be followed by an appropriate activity, such as painting, playing with clay or making collages, etc., where children can make creative use of the language learnt during the initial language game. It is only in this way that the medium-orientated language can be consolidated and become truly communicative.

The SCBP method was found to be very effective in teaching Welsh language skills at the infant stage. It has been found that, by the age of 7, listening comprehensive skills are generally well established and the majority of pupils have developed a relatively good command of spoken Welsh. However, the range of attainment in Welsh speaking skills is wider than in the case of listening comprehension (Price, 1978). The SCBP has been less successful in teaching Welsh at the junior level than at the infant level. In fact, it was noted that in some instances children's Welsh skills regressed when they entered junior school (Dodson, 1978). Several reasons are cited by Dodson (1978) and Price (1978) for the relative lack of success of the SCBP at the junior level. Teachers in the junior schools were generally less willing to devote adequate time to Welsh; fewer materials were available; teacher in-service training was inadequate; and the general approach to education in junior schools was less compatible with the aim of the project than that in infant schools—whereas the activity approach of the infant schools lends itself well to the SCBP method, the more academic verbal-written approach of the junior schools does not. In the junior schools students tend to be desk-bound and much of the communication is teacher-directed. In an attempt to provide activity-based curricular material with which Welsh could be interwoven at the junior level, the project team developed a series of special units, mostly in the area of environmental studies. However, this attempt met with only limited success as some teachers ignored or devoted insufficient time to the units while others worked on a particular unit for such a long time that children became bored.

In his summary of the evaluation report, Dodson (1978) stresses that the project was fully successful only in cases where teachers appreciated the proper sequencing of medium- and message-orientated communication. He points out that the most successful teachers were those who 'immediately followed up any medium-orientated first level work with message-orientated second level work within related or extended play activities' (1978, p. 10). The problem in many junior schools was that the focus in the Welsh sessions was predominantly on medium-orientated communication. However, in those junior schools where teachers did appreciate and respect the necessary sequencing of medium- and message-orientated communication, the results were extremely good, and many students from these schools were able to enter Welsh-medium secondary schools. In general, the SCBP approach is considered to be a promising way of helping children to become bilingual; the difficulties it faced are thought to reflect problems in implementation rather than problems in the method itself. Formal evaluation of the SCBP found that the project had no detrimental effects on children's overall academic or intellectual progress (Price, 1978).

SIGNIFICANCE OF THE SCBP

The initial methods of the SCBP with respect to the use of the second language in the classroom were considerably more cautious than those of either Canadian bilingual programmes or the Ysgolion Cymraeg. This was reflected in the relatively small amount of time devoted to the use of the second language as a medium of instruction, its confinement to peripheral subjects, and the fact that there was no formal policy regarding the teaching of Welsh reading. In general, the teaching of Welsh reading was not encouraged since a purely oral approach to the second language was considered advisable, at least until the children's proficiency in Welsh was well developed. In addition, in the initial stages of the project, structural aspects of the language played a major role in determining the syllabus. For example, structures involving the past tense were not supposed to be introduced until after the present tense had been mastered. Many of these initial methods were abandoned as the project developed. As early as 1972, a working party of the development of bilingual education in Wales suggested that the distinction between 'crucial' and 'peripheral' subjects was unnecessary (Schools Council, 1972). Teachers found that many children transferred their English reading skills to Welsh even though Welsh reading had not been explicitly taught. Similarly, many teachers found that the past tense could not be postponed until 'next term' or 'next year' if children were to be able to communicate what they wanted to say. The approach of the SCBP at the present time is much more unreservedly communicative than it was at its inception.

Although in the course of its operation many of the assumptions underlying the SCBP have moved closer to those of Canadian immersion programmes, one aspect of the SCBP experience and of Dodson's theory remains distinctive, and is potentially of both theoretical and practical significance for Canadian immersion and core second language programmes. This is the concept of systematic sequencing from medium-orientated to message-orientated communication. The relevance of this concept for immersion programmes lies in the fact that although immersion students have developed a high level of communicative competence by the end of elementary school, certain types of grammatical errors persist in their speech and have proved extremely difficult to eradicate (Adiv, 1980). In terms of Dodson's (1978) theory, these errors might be attributable to a failure to systematically integrate message-orientated communication with preliminary medium-orientated work. Although immersion students are taught linguistic structures during the French language arts period, this medium-orientated communication is isolated from the message-orientated communication that occupies the rest of the French portion of the school day. According to Dodson, medium- and message-orientated communication must be closely integrated within each teaching activity. The implication for immersion programmes is that it may be possible to avoid these linguistic errors before they become ingrained, or to rectify them once they begin to appear, through some form of medium-orientated disguised drills in the early grades. Whether or not this will prove to be the case is obviously an empirical question. A project currently underway in the Carleton Board of Education is addressed to this issue (Obadia, 1980).

Dodson's theory of second-language teaching also has considerable relevance to more conventional second-language programmes in that it shows one way in which these programmes might become more communicatively orientated without the time commitment involved in immersion. In recent years there has been much discussion of ways in which second-language syllabuses might become more functional or communicative (Van Ek, 1977; Wilkins, 1976). However, little empirical research has been carried out on what the functional needs of second language learners really are, and very few communicatively-orientated programmes have been implemented on a systematic large-scale basis. Thus, if viewed in the context of traditional programmes, Dodson's theory of second language teaching has the distinction of being one of the first communicatively-orientated theories to have been implemented on a large scale and to have been systematically evaluated. The occasional use of the learner's first language as a short-cut to meaning is an additional aspect of the SCBP approach which may be relevant to core and extended French programmes in Canada. Thus, the SCBP experience has demonstrated that an integration of medium and message, of structure and communication, and of the first and second language is possible in the context of second language programmes, and that there is a middle ground between teaching strategies which emphasize acquisition of linguistic structures divorced from students' communicative needs on the one hand, and those that emphasize message-orientated communication which is divorced from considerations of linguistic structure, on the other.

CONCLUSION

The experiences in Wales and Canada illustrate both the potential and the limitations of schools in promoting bilingualism. It is clear that bilingual programmes in both countries have met with considerable success in this regard. However, despite the fact that research has demonstrated the pedagogical soundness of the general principles underlying bilingual education for both majority and minority language students, the extent to which these programmes will continue to expand may well depend on the perception which parents have of their effectiveness in promoting general academic skills in addition to the target language.

The importance of parental perception of educational effectiveness can be seen from the Irish and Canadian experience with immersion education. In Ireland, parents' and teachers' concerns about the educational wisdom of educating children from English-speaking homes through the medium of Irish was an important factor in the decline of the number of Irish immersion schools from almost three hundred in the late 1930's to less than twenty today (Cummins, 1978). By contrast, as a result of numerous research studies, Canadian parents' perception that immersion is educationally sound has given rise to a rapid expansion of immersion programmes across Canada. Although the SCBP has been evaluated, there has otherwise been relatively little research conducted on the educational effectiveness of different forms of Welsh language instruction. The Canadian experience suggests that collection and dissemination of this type of information may be a precondition for the continued expansion of bilingual education for anglophone children in Wales. In this regard, it would seem important that parents and educators be made aware of the general educational advantages of full bilingualism and the fact that a very strong emphasis on Welsh throughout school will not detract from children's English skills.

Furthermore, while the experiences of bilingual education for anglophone children in both Wales and Canada illustrate the effectiveness with which schools can promote second language acquistion, it is also clear from both these countries that schools are much less effective in halting the long term erosion of minority languages. Mougeon and Canale (1979), for example, have argued strongly that French language schools are not sufficient to prevent the assimilation of Franco-Ontarians. Despite the presence of Quebec and the fact that French is a highly prestigious international language, the maintenance of French in Ontario, and elsewhere in English Canada, is by no means assured. Moreover, the acquisition of a second language in a school context does not necessarily guarantee its use outside school, even in bilingual communities (Genesee, 1981), so that effective pedagogical approaches to second-language teaching cannot be counted on to have immediate or direct beneficial effects for the language in the community at large.

Welsh has survived through the centuries as a result of rural isolation and the unique functions which it served within the community. In recent years, however, rural isolation has begun to break down as a result of increasing mobility and the pervasive influence of mass media, and the number of unique functions which Welsh serves in the community has declined. It appears likely that Welsh will be maintained only through a resurgence of community-wide commitment to learn *and use* the language. Although bilingual programmes are insufficient by themselves to maintain a minority language, they are clearly necessary for language maintenance and may serve as a major focus both for mobilizing a strong community-based commitment to the language and for reinforcing such a commitment through successful teaching.

REFERENCES

Adiv, E., 'An analysis of second language performance in two types of immersion programs.' Unpublished Ph.D. Thesis, Department of Education in Second Language, McGill University, 1980.

Adiv, E., and Morcos, C., *A comparison of three alternative French immersion programs at the grade 9 level,* Instructional Services, The Protestant School Board of Greater Montreal, Nov. 1979.

Bruck, M., 'The suitability of early French immersion programs for the language-disabled child', *Canadian Journal of Education,* 1978, *3,* 51-72.

Carey, S.T., and Cummins, J., *English and French achievement of grade 5 children from English, French and mixed French-English home backgrounds attending the Edmonton Separate School System English-French immersion program,* Report submitted to the Edmonton Separate School System, April 1979.

Central Advisory Council for Education (Wales), *Primary Education in Wales,* London: HMSO, 1967.

Cummins, J., 'Immersion programmes: The Irish experience', *International Review of Education,* 1978, *24,* 273- 282.

Cummins, J., and Lapkin, S., 'A survey of bilingual education programs across Canada.' In preparation.

Cziko, G., 'The effects of different French immersion programs on the language and academic skills of children from various socioeconomic backgrounds', M.A. Thesis, Department of Psychology, McGill University, 1975.

Dodson, C.J., *Language Teaching and the Bilingual Method,* Pitman, London, 1967.

Dodson, C.J., 'The Independent Evalutor's Report, in Schools Council Committee for Wales, *Bilingual Education in Wales, 5-11,* Evans/Methuen, London, 1978.

Dodson, C.J., Price, E., and Tudno Williams, I., *Towards bilingualism,* University of Wales Press, Cardiff, 1968.

Evans, E., 'Bilingual Education in Wales, in Centre for Information on Language Teaching, *Bilingualism and British Education: The Dimensions of Diversity,* CILT, London, 1976.

Genesee, F., 'The role of intelligence in second language learning', *Language Learning,* 1976, *26,* 267-280.

Genesee, F., 'A longitudinal evaluation of an early immersion school program', *Canadian Journal of Education,* 1978, *3,* 31-50.

Genesee, F., 'A comparison of early and late second language learning', *Canadian Journal of Behavioral Sciences,* 1981, in press.

Genesee, F., Polich, E., and Stanley, M.H., 'An experimental French immersion program at the secondary school level-1969 to 1974', *The Canadian Modern Language Review,* 1977, *33,* 318-322.

Genesee, F., 'Bilingualism and biliteracy: A study of cross- cultural communication in a bilingual community', in J. Edwards (Ed.), *The Social Psychology of Reading,* Silver Spring, Md., Institute of Modern Languages, 1981, 147-172.

Hébert, R., *Rendement académique et langue d'enseignement chez les élèves franco-manitobans*, Saint-Boniface, Manitoba: Centre de Recherches du Collège Universitaire de Saint-Boniface, 1976.

Morrison, F., *French proficiency: Status of Ottawa and Carleton students in alternative programs*, Research Centre, The Ottawa Board of Education, 66 Lyon Street, Ottawa, 1979.

Mougeon, R., and Canale, M., 'Maintenance of French in Ontario. Is education in French enough?' *Interchange*, 1978-79, 9, 30-39.

Obadia, A., *Analyse de fautes et techniques d'ensignement*, Le Conseil d'Education de Carleton, 1980.

Price, E., 'Bilingual education in Wales 5-11, in Schools Council Committee for Wales, *Bilingual education in Wales 5-11*, Evans, London, 1978.

Van Ek, J., *The threshold level for modern language learning in schools*, Longman, Gröningen, 1977.

Wilkins, D., *Notional syllabuses: A contribution to foreign language curriculum development*, Oxford University Press, London, 1976.

This paper derives from a study tour of bilingual schools throughout Wales by five Canadian educators in May 1979. This visit was arranged by the British Council, along with the Welsh Office, as a follow-up to a similar visit to Canadian bilingual/immersion schools in 1977 by Mr Gareth Lloyd Jones of the Welsh Office. The paper is adapted from an earlier paper entitled 'Bilingual Education: A Comparison of Welsh and Canadian Experiences' by M. Beaudoin, J. Cummins, H. Dunlop, F. Genesee and André Obadia which appeared in *The Canadian Modern Language Review*, 1981, 37, 3.

We would again like to express our appreciation to the following individuals and groups for making the study tour possible and profitable: Mr G. Fisher, Wales Representative, The British Council; Mr G. Lloyd Jones, HMI, Education Department, The Welsh Office; Oona Michaeliones, Deputy Representative, The British Council; The British Council; The Welsh Office: The British High Commission (Ottawa), and the many HMIs, principals, vice-principals and teachers who so graciously hosted us in their schools.

Schools Council Bilingual Education Project (Primary Schools) 1968-1977: An Assessment

EURWEN PRICE

AIMS OF THE BILINGUAL EDUCATION PROJECT

THE PROJECT IN BILINGUAL EDUCATION came into being in 1968, a year after the appearance of the Gittins Report.[1]* It will be seen by many to be one of the first fruits of the labours of the Gittins Committee, as it aimed at putting into practice the recommendations of the Gittins Report relating to the teaching of Welsh in anglicised areas of Wales. In paragraphs 11.3.3, 11.3.5 the report recommends that the second language should be presented to children whose mother-tongue is English as early as possible in the child's school life. Furthermore, the report advocates the establishment of a new kind of primary school, which it calls the Bilingual School, and which would introduce Welsh from the nursery stage onwards, so that the pupils would become proficient enough to allow 'systematic use of Welsh as part-medium of instruction at the junior stage'. It should be recorded here, however, that the Gittins Committee made these recommendations as a result of the testimony presented to them by people involved in Welsh education who, having observed the results of successful past experience, felt impelled to bring to the notice of the Committee the possibilities that lay waiting to be explored in setting up a systematic design for bilingual education in the primary school. The antecedents of the present Project, then, are the past examples of pioneering work whose results led indirectly to its establishment.

The task the Project set itself was the formulation of an educative programme, initially for infant schools, then leading on to activities for junior schools, which would gradually develop bilingualism by basing second-language learning firmly on the activities and experiences of the child, beginning in the reception class. This approach differs from the concept of language lessons in the traditional sense of isolating short periods of time either daily or a few times a week for teaching a language. The Project's aim was to

*For references, see page 134

51

make second-language learning, in a sense, incidental to the total educational process, because the language-learning process is grafted on to situations and activities of immediate interest to the child. This approach, it was thought, would prove to be beneficial for two reasons. In the first place it removed an objection which is sometimes voiced, namely that time devoted to teaching a second language could be better spent on other things, because the specific aim of this programme is that the child should become acquainted with the second language while he is engrossed in activities which are of educational value, whether they are used in conjunction with the first or second languages. It is of course obvious that activities aimed at developing the motor skills can without difficulty be introduced into the second-language session. But it is also true to say that the second-language session can provide valuable reinforcement of ideas and reasoning processes which need to be met in a great variety of situations before they are firmly implanted in the child's mind. One simple example, drawn from the writer's experience, will illustrate this.

The language of one-to-one distribution is usually quite familiar to the child long before he can actually put the idea into practice himself, i.e. he can say and understand the words 'one each, one for John, one for Mary, etc.' before he can distribute correctly one object to each person in a group. The ample amount of practice needed to master this skill, and in a variety of situations, can be provided by activities used in both first and second-language sessions, and the language of distribution can be mastered in two languages in the time the child has taken to acquire a firm grasp of the skill. Similar examples could be given at all intellectual levels. So the effect of the bilingual programme should be to enrich rather than to impoverish the child's general educational development. Reciprocally the teaching of the second language will benefit from its being associated so closely with activities aimed directly at the child's interests and at the correct level of his development. To implement such a programme effectively a greater part of the school day must be used than has been customary in the conventional system of language lessons. In practical terms it has been found that in the early stages of the programme the teacher begins with a limited number of situations, and the time increases gradually as the children can cope with more and more situations and activities, until about half the school day can be devoted to activities accompanied by the second language. The longer period of contact time with the second language within the school day and the variety of situations in which it can be used are both important factors in effective learning.

The linguistic content of the programme is presented in the teachers' handbook for infant schools, now published under the title *Gweithgareddau i'r Plant Bach*.[2] This contains a core of eight basic sentence structures, further broken down to provide 116 sentence patterns. These are based on 'Cymraeg Byw' and are carefully selected and graded so as to provide the child with an effective and flexible means of communication. They include the present and past, perfect and imperfect tenses of verbs, patterns of statement, question and command, a wide range of prepositions, adjectives and adverbs, and activities chosen to form the basis of the programme. These can all be found in the handbook. Any school operating this programme with imagination and flexibility should ensure that by the time they reach the top of the infant school, its pupils will have achieved a high enough level of comprehension and fluency in Welsh to enable them profitably to receive part of their instruction in the junior school through the medium of that language. Supplementary documents are available for the junior school, extending the core of language mastered in the infant school, to include for example further verb tenses and forms such as might be found in reading, comparison of adjectives and more sophisticated use of prepositions. From the top infant class onwards is laid the basis of reading skill in the second-language, first by the introduction of reading activities (e.g. substitution and sentence-making with word cards). This work is based on patterns already mastered in the oral work and in the listening books. While the oral aspect of the work receives the greatest emphasis, experience has shown that some children are eager and able to read Welsh while still in the infant school. Any child who shows a desire and ability to read in the second language is allowed and encouraged to do so. Reading skills begin to play a part in the activities of the second-language session at the junior school level, when project work entails a certain amount of reading of work-cards and even source materials.

It can be inferred from what has already been written about this programme that its preparation necessitated a careful look at the whole of the school programme, not simply from the point of view of second-language learning but also from the point of view of the children's total education. This was so for two main reasons. Firstly it was felt essential to use the time allocated to the second-language session to the utmost, and for purposes other than that simply of developing second-language skills. Secondly it was felt that to limit experience is to limit language, and the richer the educational diet could be made—intellectually, emotionally and socially—the greater would be the benefit in terms of achieving the aim of developing bilingualism. For these reasons, a range of activities has been recommended, each one of which has ample claim to be included in the school curriculum, whether associated with second-language learning or not. Included in *Gweithgareddau i'r Plant Bach* is a list of skills and concepts which can be exercised or developed by carrying out the activities recommended, while relevant activities are listed in groups after each concept.

It was felt that the transition from infant to junior work should not be made too drastic, and that infant-type activities, but at a rather more sophisticated level, could profitably be continued for part at least of the first year in the junior school, in order to prepare the children for project work to be carried out later. Then a selection of projects undertaken in the course of the junior school curriculum should ensure that the pupils cover a wide range of subject matter, mathematical, scientific, geographical, sociological, historical, religious and aesthetic. Such a programme should at the same time widen considerably the scope of their competence in the second language.

A fuller exposition of the Project's aims is included in the handbook referred to earlier, *Gweithgareddau i'r Plant Bach*. A study of this volume and the supplementary volumes which have been published will reveal the lines along which the developmental work has proceeded.

A Project such as this has a very broad base indeed in the school curriculum. While it can be said to have as one aim to lay the foundations of bilingualism in initially monoglot pupils, it sets out to do this by using an educational programme of such variety that it must set itself innumerable other goals besides. Moreover in attempting to reach them, it must lead the pupils along paths which cannot be neatly hedged about and marked out as the territory of the Bilingual Education Project alone. They may well be paths which the children will tread spurred on by other interests and stimuli provided both by school and home. The very breadth of scope the Project has allowed itself is at once a complication and a challenge. It has been considered essential to cover as broad an educational spectrum as possible, because to limit the experiential aims would mean limiting the linguistic aims as well. Against this background however, the task of evaluating achievements becomes a complicated one. Research must be the handmaiden of development and not vice versa. It would be impossible in this case, even if it were ever desirable, to tailor the developmental activities of the Project to fit a neat evaluation design. The following section will explain in which directions the research was directed.

RESEARCH AIMS

In a broad-based project with aims which often overlap areas of the curriculum not controlled by the project, it would have been impossible to attempt an objective measurement of all the educational aims. A decision had to be made about which of the Project's aims could sensibly be isolated in order to carry out a worthwhile assessment of achievement in those particular areas. It quickly became clear that there were two matters of overriding concern about which one was repeatedly questioned. One was expressed in the question 'How will this programme of bilingual education affect the pupils' general development and attainments?' The other was 'What standard of bilingualism are the pupils likely to reach after following the Project's programme?' While a host of smaller questions arose, these were undoubtedly the two big questions to which teachers and many parents clearly expected some kind of answer. They were taken as signposts pointing to the main areas of enquiry which were to be explored.

Attainment in the basic subjects
Any educational programme is likely to stand or fall in the eyes of both teachers and parents according to whether it ensures that the child can attain a satisfactory standard in the use of his mother-tongue, in reading and in mathematics, within the range of his own native ability. In an attempt to answer the question about whether a child's attainments in the basic subjects might suffer in any way if he participated in the Project, it was decided to administer a battery of tests to two year-groups of pupils, drawing samples from the top infant classes and the second-year junior classes, and to measure their attainments against those of a control group consisting of schools in Wales not participating in the Project, and similar in background and range of ability to the Project group. The tests used are listed in Appendix A (p.135), and the results of the testing programme are described in a later section of this report.

Establishing a control group
It was decided initially to establish a control group comparable in intake though not in size to the schools which made up the total Project population. First the pool of Project schools was examined to discover what types of school were present, and the following were found to be represented —

55

large city suburban schools in middle-class areas;
large council-estate schools in industrialised areas;
other urban schools of mixed intake;
urban/rural schools;
rural schools.

In order to obtain roughly the same kind of mix, eight schools were selected to form the control group, four of them being urban schools of mixed intake, and each of the other four representing one of the other categories listed above.

In the autumn of 1971 large-scale testing was carried out in the reception classes of the Project's infant schools in order to obtain a description of the ability range of the Project population and to build up a control group with a comparable ability range. The test administered was the *Primary Mental Abilities Test*[3] published by Science Research Associates. It was found that the mean scores of the two groups approximated very closely both in terms of raw scores and in terms of mental age. It was not possible to use the tables of quotient scores prepared by the test compilers, as these spanned the age-range five to seven and a half, while substantial numbers of the reception-class pupils were below five. In both Project and control groups the ages of children tested ranged from four years one month to six years. However it was possible to obtain a score based on the difference between mental and chronological age for each pupil. Testing was carried out in forty-two Project schools, yielding 787 pupils and in eight control schools, yielding 179 pupils. In terms of raw scores the mean score of the schools was 28.96 and that of the control group 28.41. In terms of differences between mental and chronological ages, both groups had, on average, a mental age between five and six months in advance of chronological age. It should be noted that the test used was standardised on samples of American children. When a t-test was carried out the difference between the two group means proved not to be statistically significant (t = 1.2986).

When the decision to test reception classes was taken it was intended to use the results for another purpose as well as to establish a comparable control group. It had been intended to treat this initial test as a pretest of the Project and control pupils who would be post-tested two or three years later and their scores examined to find out whether scoring levels had been maintained, increased or depressed, and whether there was any significant difference between Project and control groups in this respect. However for several reasons this part of the research plan had to be abandoned. In the first place, as such large numbers of pupils of such a young age were being tested, the whole of the Project team took part in test administration. In spite of the fact that prior discussion and instruction took place, it was felt that test administration had not been strictly uniform. A small proportion of the scripts had to be discarded as invalid. But even when those were excluded, it was felt that a more stringent testing procedure than had been possible in this exercise would be needed before one could with confidence use these scores in a pre- and post-test comparison. This difficulty might have been circumvented by using for testing purposes only the core of schools which had been tested by one tester who had tested the largest number of schools. However consultation with teachers and head-teachers before planning the testing of older age-groups revealed that they had a strong preference for the use of British standardised tests rather than the American test which had had to be used with the younger children. In view of these considerations it was decided to abandon the plan to administer pre- and post-tests to Project and control groups, and simply to compare the two groups at two age-levels later.

A further source of information used to compare the Project schools with the control group was the information collected about the occupations of the pupils' fathers. This was used to place the pupils into one of the following five categories —

1. professional and managerial
2. clerical, commercial and farmers
3. skilled and semi-skilled manual
4. unskilled manual
5. others e.g. father unemployed, father dead, parents separated or divorced.

The numbers and percentages of pupils in each of the five categories in both groups were as follows—

Table 1: Distribution of pupils over five categories of socio-economic background

Categories of Socio-Economic Background	Project group		Control group	
1	100	(14%)	33	(18%)
2	136	(19%)	29	(16%)
3	146	(20%)	39	(22%)
4	278	(39%)	68	(38%)
5	61	(8%)	10	(6%)

Second-language acquisition

The area of second-language acquisition can be regarded as quite specific to the Project's operation and it was naturally felt that as thorough and as objective an investigation as resources permitted was desirable in this area. There were no available tests already made for this purpose and so one major task in the research programme was to create tests of Welsh language skills suitable for administration in primary schools at both infant and junior levels. The skills of understanding, speaking, reading with understanding and, in a limited way, writing were tested. Test items whenever suitable, were first piloted using groups of native-speaking Welsh pupils, then on a trial sample of Project pupils during the year before the final testing was carried out at each age-level. As attainment in these tests cannot be measured against nationally-established norms, a descriptive account will be given later in this report of the tests themselves and of the pupils' performance in them. The tests produced were —

> a group test of listening comprehension for top infants;
> an individual oral test for top infants;
> a paper-and-pencil test of Welsh language skills for second-year juniors;
> an individual oral test for second-year juniors.

Test items are reproduced in Appendix B (p.135)

Background variables

It was decided to examine certain factors present in the pupils' background in relation to scores in the second-language tests, in an attempt to determine which, if any, exerted a significant influence on attainment.

Information relating to the top infant classes was collected about the following factors and classified into the categories described below —

> —sex of pupil
>   male
>   female
> —socio-economic background of pupil
>   (categories described above)
> —length of time pupil had followed Project programme

1. three years or more
2. two years to two years eleven months
3. one year to one year eleven months

4. less than one year
   —linguistic background of school
1. completely anglicised, with pupils unlikely ever to hear Welsh outside school
2. with a certain level of Welshness in the surrounding community, but with most pupils coming from English-speaking homes
3. with the highest level of Welshness among Project schools, some pupils having a Welsh-speaking parent, and with sometimes a Welsh stream in the school
   —amount of time in school day devoted to Project work
1. inadequate i.e. less than one hour
2. satisfactory but could be increased
3. fully adequate i.e. about half the school day.

Information relating to the second-year junior classes was collected about the following factors and classified into the categories described below —

   —sex of pupil
      male
      female
   —socio-economic background of pupil
      (categories described above)
   —linguistic background of pupil
1. neither parent speaking Welsh
2. father only speaking Welsh
3. mother only speaking Welsh.

—Project implementation in the school, taking into account time allotted, teacher attitude and preparation
1. not satisfactory
2. satisfactory.

It will be noted that the lists of factors considered in infant and junior schools are not identical. Sometimes this was due to a development in thinking as the Project proceeded. The measurement of linguistic background was made more precise at junior level and this factor was treated as a pupil variable, whereas at infant level only the level of Welsh in the community surrounding the school had been considered. The length of time the pupil had followed the Project was omitted at junior level, as the junior schools found it laborious or impossible to refer back to the infant schools. In any case results in the infant school had shown this factor to be insignificant except for very late entrants to the Project programme. At junior level late entrants were excluded from tests and the group was regarded as homogeneous in this respect. Sometimes the shifting circumstances of Project implementation made new definitions necessary. When infant schools were being considered, the time devoted to Project work was considered as one single factor, although it was recognised that it might be allied to other factors e.g. attitude. It was generally agreed in the Project team that the time allotted to Project work in the infant schools generally reflected the attitude to the Project which pervaded the school. However when Project implementation at junior level was discussed, the field officers did not feel happy to isolate the factor of time allocation. Firstly, in spite of the recommendations of the Project team, there was a general reduction of time allocated to Project work in junior schools when compared with infant schools, so that differences in time allocation were less likely to be significant. Secondly it was felt that time allocation was not as good a reflector of attitude, for example, as it had been in the infant schools. Furthermore it was clear that favourable attitude could not compensate for inadequate preparation, and although the two were often concomitant, they were not invariably so. Therefore at junior level Project implementation was regarded as a composite, made up of time allocation, teacher and head-teacher attitude and preparation. Viewed in this way schools fell fairly easily into one of the two categories, those judged to be implementing the Project satisfactorily and those where implementation clearly fell below this level.

Background information obtained from the schools and scores obtained in the tests adminstered by the Project were recorded on data sheets and then punched on cards by the Computation Centre, University College of Swansea, on whose computer the programmes of analysis were carried out.

TESTING PROGRAMME

Age-groups

It was decided to administer tests to two year-groups, one in the infant schools and the other in the junior schools. The infant school year-group was readily selected. It was judged that the last year in the infant school was the most suitable one in which to test. Test administration would be easier with the older pupils and they would have had the longest possible period of contact with the Project programme, so that a review could be made of the maximum period of time in the infant school. Also if readily available British standardised tests were to be used to measure ability and attainment in the mother-tongue then the top infant classes formed the youngest year-group it was possible to use. When selecting a year-group in the junior school it was desirable to leave as large a gap as possible between the infant and junior groups. It was also felt that the Project should avoid, where possible, testing the same cohort of pupils in two successive years so as to avoid overloading the pupils with tests. Another consideration was that the research was being carried out as the Project advanced through the primary school and it had not reached the upper classes in many of the junior schools by 1974 when the last round of tests was administered. In view of all these considerations the second year in the junior school was selected for testing. This allowed a two-year gap between the pupils tested in the top infant classes and the junior pupils tested. The two rounds of the testing programme took place in two successive years, 1973 and 1974, so that a different cohort of pupils was tested each year.

The same two year-groups were used for testing in both areas, i.e. for assessing attainment in Welsh and in the basic school subjects.

Testing ability and attainment in the basic subjects
In testing ability and attainment in the basic subjects it was decided to test English language skills, reading and mathematics and to test general ability as measured in verbal and non-verbal tests. It was not possible to do all of this, however, in the younger year-group. No acceptable tests of verbal ability or of mathematics which were suitable for group administration could be found for the top infant classes, where reading skills were not yet firmly established. A smaller battery of tests was administered to these and the full battery to the second-year junior classes. Consultation with teachers and head-teachers confirmed the opinion that it was desirable to select tests that had been standardised on samples of British schoolchildren. It was found that tests published by the National Foundation for Educational Research were acceptable to all concerned and so it was from these that the final batteries of tests were selected. The Foundation will henceforth be referred to in this report by its initials NFER.

The following NFER tests were administered to pupils of 7 and over in top infant classes in 1973:

> *Picture Test A*
> *Reading Test BD*
> *English Progress Test A2*

The following tests were administered to second-year junior pupils in 1974:

Mathematics Test B
Reading Test BD
English Progress Test B2
Non-Verbal Ability Test BD
Verbal Ability Test BC

Each of the test batteries was administered to two samples of eight schools, one drawn from the pool of Project schools, the other forming a control group. The nature of these samples is described in the section 'Sampling procedures' (v. p.63). Results of the comparisons made are described in the section 'Testing Project and control groups in the infant schools' (v. p.67) and 'Testing Project and control groups in the junior schools' (v. p.69).

Testing Welsh language skills
In order to test language skills in Welsh, two tests were prepared for each age-group. In the infant schools the Project had laid emphasis on understanding and speaking the second language and had not formulated any policy of training the pupils in reading and writing at this stage, so the tests prepared for the infants were designed to test only the skills of comprehension and speech. A listening comprehension test called *Prawf Gwrando a Deall* was devised, consisting of picture booklets accompanied by a tape. This test was designed for group administration and was administered to all Project pupils in top infant classes in a total of 34 schools. A detailed description of the construction of this test is given in the section 'Constructing a listening test for infants' (v. p.73). An analysis of the scores obtained and factors affecting the scores can be found in the section *'Prawf Gwrando a Deall,* 1973' (v. p.77).

An oral test was also devised for administration to individual pupils in this age-group. The length of time required to administer such a test meant that only a sample of schools could take part in this test. It was decided to use the same sample of eight schools as was drawn for administering the NFER tests. This test is described in the section 'Constructing an oral test for infants' (v. p.82). Scores in this test are examined in the section *'Prawf Llafar,* 1973' (v. p.87).

For the nine-year-old pupils a paper-and-pencil group test was devised called *Prawf Cymraeg.* This was administered to all Project pupils in the twenty schools where the Project had reached the second year junior level. This test is described in the section

'Constructing a Welsh test for juniors' (v. p.93). The results of this test are examined in the section *'Prawf Cymraeg, 1974'* (v. p.97). An oral test was also administered to a sample of the junior pupils. This tests is described in the section 'An oral test for juniors' (v. p.107). The sample obtained for this test was of a different kind from the one obtained for the infant oral test and is described in the section 'Sampling procedures' below.

The final testing programme was carried out in the latter half of the school sessions 1972-73 and 1973-74. The Welsh group tests were administered in all schools within a period of about two weeks near the end of the Easter term. In the infant schools the administration of the NFER test and the Welsh oral test occupied the whole of the summer term in 1973. In the junior schools the Welsh oral testing had also to take place before Easter as the longer battery of NFER tests administered to the juniors occupied the whole of the summer term in 1974.

SAMPLING PROCEDURES

The schools participating in the Bilingual Education Project were not obtained by means of any form of sampling procedure. When the Project was first set up, and at later stages in its life, schools were nominated by local education authorities for a variety of reasons, and began their period of co-operation with the Project team with varying degrees of enthusiasm for the exercise they were about to undertake. The pool of schools obtained in this way consisted mainly of urban schools of mixed intake, but also contained large city schools in middle-class areas, large urban schools in industrial areas drawing pupils exclusively from council estates, urban/rural schools and purely rural schools. They were scattered throughout Wales in all except two of the local education authorities that existed before the re-organisation of 1974. They were not, of course, situated in the most Welsh areas, where Welsh is the first language and natural medium of instruction in the primary schools. The total group must be regarded, in sampling terms, as a population and not as a sample. From this population samples had to be drawn for certain parts of the testing programme.

Samples for testing general attainment

The section of this report entitled 'Research aims' has already described how an initial description of the Project population was obtained in 1971-1972 by means of testing reception classes and examining the socio-economic background of the pupils as reflected in the occupations of the fathers. In the same way a small control group was established, consisting of eight schools similar in background and ability to the Project population. The control group was needed for the purpose of measuring the general attainments of a sample of Project pupils against those of a control group not associated with the Project. As it was not possible to test all the Project schools for general attainment in the two year-groups chosen, a sample of eight schools was drawn from the pool of Project schools, to undergo the same battery of tests as was to be administered to the control group. Separate Project samples were obtained for the two year-groups, i.e. top infants and second-year juniors.

The Project samples were obtained in the following way. First the scores obtained by all Project schools in the Primary Mental Abilities Test were examined. Although there was no significant difference between the mean scores of both groups, the range of scores in the Project schools, both individual scores and school means, was wider than that of the smaller group of control schools. In order to avoid the possibility of the Project sample's not reflecting accurately the distribution of the control group, if for example a disproportionate number fell at the extremes of the scoring range, a cluster sample was taken. The school means of the control group were examined, the range extended upwards and downwards by two points each way, and only the Project schools which clustered within that range were included in the sampling pool. Also excluded, of course, were schools where the Project had not yet reached the top infant classes, in the case of the 1973 sample, and the second-year junior classes, in the case of the 1974 sample.

As the control group had included examples of the same types of school as those present in the Project population, the 'cluster' which now formed the pool of Project schools was next categorised in the same way and the requisite number of schools from each category was then selected randomly from the number available. Both the control group and the Project sample now contained eight schools as follows —

> 4 urban schools of mixed intake;
> 1 large city suburban school;
> 1 large urban school with a council-estate intake;
> 1 urban/rural school;
> 1 rural school.

In order that standardised scores might be used, the scores of all pupils in the top infant classes who had not had their seventh birthday by the day of testing were excluded when comparisons were made of the performance of Project and control groups in the NFER tests of attainment and general ability. In the case of the *English Progress Test* pupils under seven years and three months had to be excluded.

The socio-economic background of the Project and control groups tested at infant level in 1973 was examined, and the pupils placed in the five categories described in the section entitled 'Research aims.' The numbers and percentages of pupils in each category are shown in the following table.

Table 2: Distribution of infants tested in 1973 over five categories of socio-economic background

Categories of Socio-Economic Background	Project group		Control group	
1	25	(18%)	34	(21%)
2	33	(23%)	32	(20%)
3	33	(23%)	45	(28%)
4	40	(28%)	49	(30%)
5	10	(7%)	2	(1%)

The same examination was made of the socio-economic background of the Project and control groups tested in the junior school in 1974. The group of control schools remained the same, although a different pupil cohort was used. A new Project sample of eight schools was drawn, using the same procedure as that described above. The number and percentage of pupils in each category are shown in the following table.

Table 3: Distribution of junior pupils tested in 1974 over five categories of socio-economic background

Categories of Socio-economic Background	Project group		Control group	
1	26	(13%)	49	(18%)
2	36	(18%)	53	(20%)
3	54	(26%)	78	(30%)
4	77	(38%)	73	(28%)
5	11	(5%)	11	(4%)

Second-language testing

At both infant and junior levels the group tests of Welsh language skills were administered to the whole of the year-group in all schools where the Project had reached the relevant year-group. The listening comprehension test *(Prawf Gwrando a Deall)* was administered to top infant classes in thirty-four schools and the Welsh language test for juniors *(Prawf Cymraeg)* was administered to second-year junior classes in twenty schools.

Testing oral skills was a more lengthy procedure which necessitated individual testing, so for this purpose only samples could be tested. In testing the infants, it was decided to use the sample of eight schools which had been drawn for the administration of NFER tests, and the Welsh oral tests were administered, wherever possible, to all pupils in the year-group. In one large school the time schedule did not allow all pupils to be tested so a random selection was made of the number of pupils who could be tested in the time available. It was possible to carry out the test in two further schools in the course of subsequent school visits, making a total of ten schools in which the oral test was administered.

In administering the junior school oral tests a different strategy was adopted. It was felt desirable to administer a much longer oral test to the junior pupils, and so the number of pupils tested had to be considerably reduced. In order not to restrict unduly the number of schools visited for this purpose it was decided to administer the test in ten of the twenty schools which were to do the group test, and within those ten schools to test a small sample of pupils drawn from three bands of linguistic ability, above-average, average and below-average. In this way linguistic profiles of each of these three bands could be built up based on pupil response in the various units of the oral test. It was decided also to administer some of the units to a small sample of Welsh-speaking pupils in order to be able to compare some of the linguistic features of the speech of nine-year-old pupils who had followed the Project programme with those of Welsh-speaking pupils of similar age. The native Welsh speakers were obtained from one Welsh school in an anglicised town and one traditional Welsh school in rural Wales.

Numbers of pupils tested

Tables 4 and 5 below show the numbers of pupils to whom NFER tests of ability and attainment were administered.

Table 4: Numbers of infant pupils to whom NFER tests were administered.

Test	No. of pupils in Project group	No. of pupils in control group
Picture Test A	143	164
Reading Test BD	143	164
English Progess Test A2	91	98

Table 5: Numbers of junior pupils to whom NFER tests were administered.

Test	No. of pupils in Project group	No. of pupils in control group
Mathematics Test B	206	275
Reading Test BD	207	280
English Progress Test B2	207	280
Non-Verbal Ability Test BD	204	281
Verbal Ability Test BC	205	275

Table 6 below shows the numbers of schools involved and the numbers of pupils included in the testing of Welsh language skills at both infant and junior levels.

Table 6: Numbers of pupils to whom Welsh language tests were administered.

Test	Level	No. of schools	No. of pupils
Prawf Gwrando a Deall	Infant	34	704
Prawf Llafar	Infant	10	149
Prawf Cymraeg	Junior	20	427
Prawf Llafar	Junior	10	40

TESTING PROJECT AND CONTROL GROUPS

Infant-school testing
During the summer term of 1973 tests of general ability and of attainment in English and reading were administered to a sample of

eight Project schools and eight control schools. No satisfactory group test of mathematical attainment could be found for this age group. Reading skills could not be regarded as having been firmly enough established to justify the use of a mathematical test which depended largely on such skills. Individual oral tests would have been too lengthy to administer. Therefore it was decided to defer the testing of mathematical ability and, for the same reasons, verbal ability until the junior classes were tested in 1974. The following test battery was administered in the sixteen schools—

NFER *Picture Test A* (non-verbal ability)
NFER *Reading Test BD*
NFER *English Progress Test A2*

The first two tests were administered to all pupils in the top infant classes who were seven years old and over on the day of testing. The third was administered to all pupils who were seven years and three months and over on the day of testing. These age limits were strictly adhered to in order that standardised scores could be used. The number of pupils tested on the English Progress Test was thus smaller than the numbers tested on the other two tests.

Mean scores were calculated for both groups and a comparison of means was made for each test, using 't' values [4] to measure the significance of the difference between the means. The following tables summarise the results.

Table 7: Comparison of performance of Project and control groups of infants in Picture Test A.

	Project group	Control group
No. of pupils	143	164
Range of scores	75—137	80—140
Mean score	108.30	107.85
Standard deviation	12.0605	13.4020

t = 1 . 60   - No significant difference

Table 8: Comparison of performance of Project and control groups of infants in Reading Test BD

	Project group	Control group
No. of pupils	143	164
Range of scores	74—128	73—140
Mean score	100.25	100.82
Standard deviation	13.2931	14.8089

t = 1 . 79   - No significant difference

Table 9: Comparison of performance of Project and control groups of infants in English Progress Test A2

	Project group	Control group
No. of pupils	91	98
Range of scores	77—131	76—132
Mean score	103.56	102.77
Standard deviation	12.0194	14.7872

t = 0 . 98   - No significant difference

The results obtained in comparing these two groups do not suggest that the implementation of the Bilingual Education Project has had any observable effect on achievement in English and reading, or on the development of the pupils' general ability.

Junior-school testing
During the summer of 1974 the same kind of comparison was made of Project and control groups as had been carried out among top infant classes in 1973. This time the pupils who took part in the testing programme were those about to complete the second year in the junior schools. The programme was not an exact replication of the previous year's programme, as difficulties which had presented themselves in testing seven-year-olds in certain areas e.g. mathematics and verbal ability, were no longer present for the junior pupils, so that a larger battery of tests could be used. Five NFER tests were administered in each school. They were—

> *Reading Test BD*
> *English Progress Test B2*
> *Mathematics Test B* (orally administered)

Non-verbal Ability Test BD
Verbal Ability BC

The tests were again administered in eight Project and eight control schools. The same control group as had been used in 1973 was again used in 1974. It consisted of either the junior departments of the same schools or the junior schools to which the infants had proceeded. It was decided, however, in the interests of fairness and in order to increase confidence in the results, to draw another sample of eight schools from the Project group, using the same procedure as before.

The samples tested in 1974 were considerably larger than those tested in 1973, although the same number of schools was used. In the top infant classes only pupils who had had their seventh birthday at the time of testing were tested, so that standardised scores could be used. This excluded about one-third of the pupils in the year-group and about 300 pupils were tested altogether. In 1974 there was no necessity for excluding any of the pupils in the year-group because of age, and about 480 pupils were tested altogether. In the Project group the scores of pupils who had recently transferred to a Project school, and who therefore did not represent Project pupils, were excluded from the comparison of mean scores.

When the socio-economic background of the two groups to be tested in 1974 was examined, it was felt that the two distributions were not as well matched as it had been hoped they would be. The following table shows the number and percentage of pupils in each category of socio-economic background in all Project schools surveyed in 1971, in the Project sample tested in 1974 and in the control group tested in 1974.

Table 10: Distribution over 5 categories of socio-economic background of 1971 Project population and 1974 samples

Socio-economic background	All Project schools in 1971		Project sample 1974		Control group 1974	
1	100	(14%)	26	(13%)	49	(18%)
2	136	(19%)	36	(18%)	53	(20%)
3	146	(20%)	54	(26%)	78	(30%)
4	278	(39%)	77	(38%)	73	(28%)
5	61	(8%)	11	(5%)	11	(4%)

It can be seen that the Project sample used in 1974 is a fairly faithful reflection of the total population of Project schools surveyed in 1971. However the control group in 1974 shows a slightly different distribution over the socio-economic background scale from that of the Project sample, with a slight weighting in the higher categories, whereas the Project sample shows more weight in category 4. The main reason for the difference was that in the control group a large number of pupils in the city suburban school had to be tested in order to include the full ability range. In the Project school of similar type and size only one class in the year-group followed the Bilingual Project, parental choice being the basis for entry into the bilingual stream. It follows that this school yielded much smaller numbers than did its partner in the control group. In view of this imbalance it was judged wise to carry out the comparison of mean scores within categories of socio-economic background, and not simply to compare the two groups as was done in 1973.

The following table shows the mean scores in each test of the Project pupils, within categories of socio-economic background.

Table 11: Mean scores of Project pupils in 5 tests within categories of socio-economic background

Socio-economic background	Reading	Maths	English	Non-Verbal	Verbal
1	110.38	107.36	112.76	112.65	112.92
2	102.22	98.82	106.41	102.27	102.97
3	101.61	99.09	105.52	101.71	102.71
4	94.85	95.15	101.47	96.89	97.09
5	92.45	94.40	97.00	94.81	94.70

The following table shows the mean scores in each test of the control group, within categories of socio-economic background.

71

Table 12: Mean scores of control group pupils in 5 tests within categories of socio-economic background

Socio-economic background	Reading	Maths	English	Non-Verbal	Verbal
1	107.50	104.10	111.30	111.37	108.37
2	103.50	99.82	107.42	102.33	104.21
3	101.06	97.87	104.42	102.01	101.93
4	96.94	94.88	99.89	99.83	97.45
5	96.81	98.30	98.36	102.00	100.70

The differences between the means of Project and control group pupils within each category of socio-economic background were examined and a t-value ⁴ obtained to measure the significance of the difference. The following table shows the t-values obtained.

Table 13: t- values obtained to compare differences between Project and control group means in 5 tests within 5 categories of socio-economic background

Socio-economic background	Reading	Maths	English	Non-Verbal	Verbal
1	1.18	1.25	0.66	0.39	2.01*
2	0.53	0.39	0.38	0.02	0.52
3	0.25	0.63	0.54	0.12	0.39
4	0.96	0.07	0.73	1.32	0.19
5	0.67	0.67	0.29	1.23	1.33

* Significant at 5% level

It can be seen that only one of these t-values reveals a significant difference, and that only at the five per cent level. The performance of the Project pupils of the highest socio-economic category in the test of verbal ability would seem to be significantly better than that of the control group pupils in the same socio-economic category. The other categories of social background, however, do not reveal any significant difference. In fact twenty-four out of the twenty-five t-values show no significant difference between the two groups. The presence of one significant difference in one category of pupils only may of course be due, not to the influence of the Project, but to the presence of some hidden factor undetected by this enquiry. However the finding is an interesting one, and if further research showed it to recur persistently, it would suggest that a sharpening of the verbal intelligence of the socially advantaged might be a by-product of a programme of bilingual education. However in the context of the present testing programme we must remind ourselves that this particular superiority did not have any carry-over effect on attainment in the tests supposedly linked with verbal ability. Performance in reading and English was not significantly different in the two groups.

Overall one must conclude that there is little if any significant difference in general ability or in attainment in English and mathematics between the Project pupils and their contemporaries in the control group. The results obtained in 1974 reinforce, and on a wider front, those obtained in 1973, and can only increase confidence in the belief that the Bilingual Education Project does not result in any lowering of standards of general attainment in infant or in junior schools.

CONSTRUCTING A LISTENING COMPREHENSION TEST FOR INFANTS

A listening comprehension test was considered to be an important component of the second-language testing to be carried out in top infant classes. Aural and oral skills are the ones on which greatest emphasis is placed in the infant schools and so it was felt that these two skills should be tested before the Project pupils proceeded to the junior schools. Since oral tests are so time-consuming in administration, the oral test was administered to only a sample of the Project pupils in this age-group. A listening comprehension test however, devised for easy group administration, was used to assess the standard of second-language attainment in this particular skill in all the Project schools.

The test consisted of a tape on which the test items were recorded, to be played to a group, and individual booklets containing strips of four pictures, which the pupils marked to indicate their response. The basis of the linguistic content of the test items was the material provided or recommended for use in the infant classes, both the language of the listening books and the language which would normally accompany the range of other activities referred to in *Gweithgareddau i'r Plant Bach*. However the very form of the test imposed its own limitations on the linguistic content of the test. Certain structural features which are learnt in the infant schools had to be excluded (e.g. the first and second person forms of verbs, the imperfect tense) because they could not be presented pictorially with the clarity and absence of ambiguity necessary in material used for testing. Not only had each element to be capable of clear pictorial representation, but also the contrast between the crucial element and the alternatives had likewise to be capable of the same unambiguous presentation. In consequence only twelve types of sentence were represented in the test. Here are examples, taken from the test material, of each one of the twelve types:

> Mae'r defaid yn y gorlan.
> Mae'r plant yn clirio'r eira.
> Dydy'r fuwch ddim yn y beudy.
> Dydy'r morlo ddim yn nofio yn y llyn.
> Mae llestri yn y cwpwrdd.
> Does dim het ar y dyn eira.
> Does dim mwg yn dod allan o'r simnai.
> Mae Mair wedi agor y drws.
> Dydy'r plant ddim wedi gwisgo i fyny.
> Mae e'n bwyta hufen ia.
> Maen nhw wyneb i waered.
> Dyma'r brws paent.

By varying the vocabulary used, a set of 120 test items was devised. A word-count of the examples of parts of speech used showed that the test material contained 118 nouns, two pronouns, forty-two verbs, eighteen adjectives, five adverbs, eleven prepositions and three numerals.

A number of the adjectives included were adjectives of colour. It was considered desirable to test these as colour is such an important feature of materials used in infant classes. This decision made it necessary to produce at least part of the test in colour. To avoid undue expense it was decided to isolate the items making reference to colour and to include them in a short test of twenty items (*Prawf Gwrando a Deall* A) for which coloured booklets were printed, and to produce black-and-white booklets containing the remaining 100 items (*Prawf Gwrando a Deall* B). Thus 480 pictures were commissioned to make up the 120 picture strips. The pupils were required to mark in each strip the picture which corresponded to the tape-recorded item they heard. The positioning of the 'correct' picture in each strip was determined by using a table of random numbers.

With the help of the National Language Unit at Pontypridd, a tape was made to accompany each booklet. Tape A consisted of twenty phrases, not sentences, and tape B of 100 sentences. The test was split into two roughly equal parts and administered in two sessions with a break in between. Because of regional differences of vocabulary and accent two versions of the tapes were made, one for use in north Wales and one for use in south Wales.

The first stage of piloting this material consisted of administering the tests to seventy pupils in the top infant classes of three Welsh-medium primary schools, one of these being a rural school in Pembrokeshire and the other two Welsh schools in anglicised areas. The purpose of this was to identify any ambiguity in the pictures used. The percentage of correct response to each item was obtained. In test A, between eighty and one hundred per cent of the pupils responded correctly to sixteen of the twenty items. In test B, between eighty and one hundred per cent of the pupils responded correctly to seventy-six of the hundred items. The remaining items were examined carefully to try to determine the reasons for their failure to elicit substantially uniform response from these pupils. In the case of test A it was felt that only one item failed because of ambiguity in the picture strip. This was easily located and amended. The other three presented some difficulty even to native speakers in this age-group. The difficulty was either one of vocabulary ('gleiniau') or one of auditory discrimination ('blodau' and 'blodyn') or one which arose from a combination of grammatical and aural difficulties ('tair cath fach' and 'cregyn'). 'Tair' was interpreted as 'dau' by some of the pupils living in anglicised areas. This confusion was doubtless caused by the inability, clearly revealed in the oral test, of some children in this type of area to make the distinction between the masculine and feminie forms of numerals. 'Cregyn' was clearly thought by some to be a singular and not a plural form. In test B the pictures accompanying five of the items were found to be unclear or ambiguous. The remaining items with lower item scores however were felt to prevent some difficulty, either lexical or syntactic. About half of these contained rather difficult vocabulary e.g. 'corlan', 'coelcerth', 'wyneb i waered', while the others were negative sentences.

In order further to test this material on a sample of Project pupils, a sample of thirteen schools was used, one school being randomly chosen to represent each LEA participating in the Project. The tests were manually scored and then responses were recorded on data forms. These were sent to the Computation Centre of the University College of Swansea, accompanied by programming instructions to yield the following information about each test:

individual pupil scores;

rank-ordered scores within schools and within the samples;

a mean score, variance and standard deviation within schools and within samples;

a facility value for each item (percentage of correct response);

a discrimination value for each item (based on item response in top and bottom thirds);

a reliability coefficient obtained by using the Kuder-Richardson formula 20.

The following table summarises the test results.

Table 14: Results of pilot testing of Prawf Gwrando a Deall *in Project schools.*

	Gwrando a Deall A	Gwrando a Deall B
Number of pupils tested	296	296
Number of items tested	20	100
Range of scores	2—20	12—96
Mean score	13.48	65.32
Standard deviation	4.03	18.12
Reliability coefficient	0.76	0.94

The coefficient of reliability was predictably lower for the twenty-item test than for the longer one. Parts A and B were dealt with as separate tests because the computer programme used had been previously designed to deal with tests containing up to 100 items. It was decided to include fifty items in the final version of the test, including some from test A and some from test B.

The distribution of scores for the Project sample reflected the fact that the pilot version of the listening comprehension test was too easy and that the final version of the test needed to be stiffened. For test A the facility values ranged from 37.76 to 93.20. For test B they ranged from 23.13 to 96.94. In selecting items for the final version care was taken to achieve a better balance between the numbers of easy and difficult items. The following criteria were used in selecting items for the final test:

to use only items with facility values falling within the range of 25.00 to 75.00;

to use only items with discrimination values greater than 0.30;

to discard all items judged unsuitable as a result of the pilot test on native speakers, i.e. those with unclear or ambiguous pictures.

Seven items were chosen from test A and forty-three from test B. A further six easy items from test B were included as practice items. The items selected, together with the facility value and discrimination value of each, are listed in Appendix B (1), which also includes a sample of the picture booklet used in the final form of the test.

In the final version of the test, parts A and B were reversed, as it was noticed during the pilot tests that pupils who did test B first found it easier to master the mechanics of the test in a short time than those who did test A first. This was felt to be because the longer sentence stimuli on the test tape B conveyed meaning more easily than the shorter phrases on the test tape A. Pupils who did test B first generally learned to do what was required of them within the space of two or three items, and then proceeded without difficulty to test A. So the longer black-and-white booklet was re-named *Gwrando a Deall A,* while the shorter coloured booklet was re-named *Gwrando a Deall B.*

PRAWF GWRANDO A DEALL

During the Easter term of 1973 the listening comprehension test, *Prawf Gwrando a Deall,* was administered to 704 pupils in thirty-four schools, i.e. all the schools in which the Project was operating in the top infant classes. Part A and B were regarded as one test and the whole was scored out of fifty. The mean score of the whole group was twenty-eight and the scores ranged from zero to forty-nine. However, scores were examined within each of four categories into which pupils had been classified according to the length of time they had followed the Project's bilingual programme. The following table summarises the results.

Table 15: Prawf Gwrando a Deall *results within 4 categories*

Length of time pupils had followed Project	No. of scores	Mean score	Standard deviation
1. 3 yrs. or more	58	29.24	10.65
2. 2 yrs. to 2 yrs. 11 mths.	305	30.37	10.09
3. 1 yr. to 1 yr. 11 mths.	295	29.77	9.83
4. Less than 1 yr.	46	21.78	10.11

All the pupils tested, however long they had followed the Project programme, were at the same level in their infant schools, and all were tested within a period of one fortnight, a little more than one term before they were to proceed to their junior schools. The similarity between the mean scores of the first three categories seems to suggest that their teachers had aimed at a certain level of attainment and ensured that their pupils reached it before leaving the infant school, regardless of the length of time they had followed a bilingual programme. The two largest categories roughly equal in size, attained mean scores that are less than one point apart, and the pupils who had followed the Project for the longest time had a mean score very slightly below that of the pupils who were still in their second year of the Project programme. Only the very late entrants to the Project, those who had transferred from the other schools, had a substantially lower mean score in this test, and even these had reached a commendable level of comprehension when it is remembered that most had followed a programme of bilingual education for only two terms. Setting this last category aside, it would appear that whether bilingual education was carried on for two years or for three in the infant school, the level of attainment, as far as comprehension of the second language is concerned, was roughly the same. That there were differences between schools was clear when school means were computed and found to range from seventeen to forty out of fifty. There was even evidence of within-school difference. Factors accounting for these differences will be referred to later.

A series of chi-square tests was carried out using scores in *Prawf Gwrando a Deall* and categories of variables relating to the background of the pupil or the school. Contingency tables from which chi-square values were obtained are reproduced in Appendix D (p.152). The scores of the whole group were used to obtain the values of chi-square seen in Table 16 opposite, when relating the scores of the three pupil variables of sex, socio-economic back-ground and the time the pupil had followed the Project.

The high level of significance of the chi-square value obtained in examining categories of time the pupils had followed the Project in relation to their scores is attributable to the distribution of the scores of the late entrants and not to any noticeable differences between the other categories, as has been explained in the earlier part of this section.

Table 16: Values of chi-square obtained from relating 3 pupil variables to scores in Prawf Gwrando a Deall

	Value of chi-square	d.f.	Level of significance
Sex			
Socio-economic	1.45	2	Not significant
background	15.45	8	Not significant
Time pupil had			
followed Project	27.85	6	0.001

There is no marked difference between the score distributions of boys and girls in this test, so that sex does not have any significant influence on performance in the comprehension test.

The distribution of scores when related to socio-economic background does reveal a tendency for pupils in the highest category of social background to achieve high scores and for pupils in category five, i.e. either pupils whose fathers were unemployed, or dead, or those whose parents were separated, to achieve low scores. However the overall distribution of scores does not quite reach a level of significance, even at the level of 0.05.

Two variables related to the school were examined within the two largest categories of 'time the pupil had followed the Project,' although as it turned out there was little difference between the performance of these two categories. The two variable were the linguistic background of the school and the amount of time devoted to Project work during the school day. The smaller categories of 'time the pupil had followed the Project' were ignored as these were exceptional groups and therefore of less relevance than the two main categories of pupils who had followed the Project without interruption for just under three years and just under two years respectively. The following tables show the chi-square values obtained in examining these two variables in relation to test scores within the two categories.

Table 17: Values of chi-square obtained from relating 2 school variables to scores of third-year pupils in Prawf Gwrando a Deall

	Value of chi-square	d.f.	Level of significance
Linguistic			
background	6.43	4	Not significant
Time devoted			
to Project	28.98	4	0.001

Table 18: Values of chi-square obtained from relating 2 school variables to scores of second-year pupils in Prawf Gwrando a Deall

	Value of chi-square	d.f.	Level of significance
Linguistic background	6.63	4	Not significant
Time devoted to Project	28.23	4	0.001

When the schools' linguistic background was considered the values of chi-square obtained in both groups of pupils were very similar, neither of them reaching a level of significance. This result suggests that the level of Welshness of the school and its surrounding community has no significant influence on levels of attainment in understanding Welsh.

When the amount of time devoted to the Project in the school day was considered, again the values of chi-square obtained in both groups were very similar, but this time they reached a high level of significance. The distribution of scores indicates that the category judged to devote clearly inadequate time to the Project programme had a marked tendency to low achievement, while the largest proportion of high scores was found in schools judged to devote fully adequate time.

It is strongly felt that another variable very likely to influence pupil achievement is the attitude of teachers and head teachers towards the implementation of the Project. However, this was a difficult variable to categorise for more than one reason. The area of attitude is a delicate one to chart, particularly so in this case, as attitude towards bilingual education in Wales is often closely bound up with attitudes towards the Welsh language, which in their turn often have emotional overtones, deriving from social, political and even religious background. It was felt that people would be unwilling to commit their attitudes towards the Project too precisely to paper, on a questionnaire form for example, because they might feel, not unnaturally, that they were revealing too much of themselves if they did so. It is generally felt that the attitude of the head teacher is extremely important, and can, if favourable, inspire the members of staff to commitment to such a Project and support them in its implementation. It was judged that the amount of time devoted to the Project in the school day would probably reflect the school's general attitude towards the Project, and that this variable would be the nearest approximation possible to a measure of attitude. However it must be recognised that the approximation is a very rough one. While recognising the importance and weight of the head teacher's attitude, one must also admit that it is not necessarily all-pervasive, and that each individual staff member has his or her own individual attitude and opinions. Furthermore, pupils are exposed to the attitudes of different teachers in successive years and achievement could not be classified as being influenced by one undiluted type of attitude. It is even possible that teacher attitude may change, for better or for worse, over a period of two or three years. Indeed instances of this have occured during the period of operation of the Project. The difference that can occur within a school was dramatically illustrated by one school in which two top infant classes were tested. One had been taught in the year of testing by a teacher whose attitude towards the Project was very favourable. The other had been taught during this year by a teacher whose attitude was frankly and markedly less favourable. The group taught by the favourable teacher had an average score of thirty-seven out of fifty, while the other group had an average score of fifteen out of fifty. Both groups were judged by the head teacher to have roughly the same range of ability, and both had received the same teaching in the years preceding the top infant class.

It was not possible to test all the Project schools for general ability and attainment in the first language, but this was done in a sample of eight schools, for the purpose of comparing the attainments of Project pupils with those of a control group. The scores of the Project group in the general ability and reading tests were also used to examine the relationship between attainment in these tests and attainment in *Prawf Gwrando a Deall*. The results are shown in the table below.

Table 19: Values of chi-square obtained from relating scores in 2 NFER tests to scores in Prawf Gwrando a Deall

	Value of chi-square	d.f.	Level of significance
Picture Test A	14.64	4	0.01
Reading Test BD	6.45	4	Not significant

The chi-square value of 14.64 suggests that there is some correlation between ability as measured in *Picture Test A* and performance in the Welsh comprehension test. It should be noted that the format and procedure of these two tests were very similar. Each consisted of a picture booklet and spoken questions and all items were of the multiple-choice variety. The other value of chi-square, 6.45, suggests that there is little relationship between performance in the English reading test and the Welsh comprehension test.

Two conclusions may be drawn from this examination of *Prawf Gwrando a Deall* scores:

1. that the level of general ability of the individual is likely to affect his level of comprehension of the second language;
2. that as far as the school's administration of the Project is concerned, the amount of time devoted to Project work in the school day is a crucial factor in successful acquisition of comprehension skills in the second language, the greater amount of time being associated with high achievement.

It is probably also true to say that teacher attitude towards and commitment to the idea of bilingual education has a strong bearing on levels of pupil achievement.

CONSTRUCTING AN ORAL TEST FOR INFANTS

It was felt essential to devise some form of oral test as part of the second-language test for the top infant classes. To test listening comprehension alone would be to ignore a very important area of language mastery, i.e. oral skill, and one on which the whole programme of the Project laid especial emphasis. Several types of oral production test were examined and considered. Taking into account the age of the pupils, the need for reliability, ease of scoring and ease and speed of administration, it was felt that the best form of test for the present purpose would be one similar in form to the grammatical closure sub-test of the *Illinois Test of Psycholinguistic Ability*.[5] The test devised consisted of thirty-five items initially, each item being illustrated by a pair of pictures specially drawn for the purpose. The first picture was described by the tester, who then asked the pupil to say something about the second picture. The aim was to relate the picture in each pair so closely, either in similarity, contrast or sequence, that the same or a similar response would be elicited from each pupil. The piloting of this test was carried out in two stages. First the items were administered to native-speakers of Welsh in the same age-group as the target population for whom the test was intended. This stage provided an assessment of the efficiency of the pictures in eliciting the intended response. A secondary purpose was served, too, in providing some indication of the standard of response among Welsh-speaking pupils, which could be compared with the standard of response of the Project pupils. At the next stage, items which had proved satisfactory in the initial piloting were administered to a sample of pupils from Project schools. The thirty-five items used in the initial pilot test are listed in Appendix B(2) (p.138).

Pilot test among native speakers
The test was tried out on a sample of sixty-seven pupils from three schools, one being a traditional Welsh school in rural Pembrokeshire, the other two being Welsh schools in anglicised areas. All responses were recorded on tape and transcripts made. In order to test the effectiveness of the pictures in eliciting the required response, a record was made of how many pupil responses corresponded to the expected response for each item of the test. Nineteen of the items succeeded in eliciting the expected response from over three-quarters of the sample. In the case of twelve of the nineteen items, ninety-one to one hundred per cent of the pupils gave the expected response. The pictures with the highest scores for consistent response were judged suitable for inclusion in the second stage of piloting to be carried out on a sample drawn from Project schools.

Responses to the remaining items were then examined in order to try to establish reasons for their failure to elicit the required response. The reasons fell into two categories:

— there was great variety of response when the pictures provided were ambiguous, i.e. suggested more than one interpretation or line of thought to the pupils;
— there was simplified or incorrect response, or failure to respond, when the item itself proved to be linguistically difficult even for pupils who were native speakers of Welsh.

Items which fell into the first category obviously had to be excluded. However the five items which fell into the second category were included in the second pilot test, in order that observations might be made about the degree of difficulty they presented to children in the Project schools. Four items proved so unsatisfactory that they were omitted after they had been used in the first class of thirty-four pupils. One other item was amended at

83

an early stage in an attempt to make it more efficient.

In the course of testing, a number of interesting observations were made about the influence of certain factors on response.

1. The difficulty of using pictures to convey verb tenses was underlined by this test. Three items required a substitution of past for present. Only one of them proved satisfactory—'Mae hi wedi torri'i gwallt'. In one item the picture was unclear and in the other many of the pupils succeeded in giving correct and sensible response without using the past tense at all.

2. It was extremely difficult to elicit plural forms of nouns, as whenever the number of objects in the picture was easily countable, the children stated the number of objects portrayed, and so in Welsh used the singular noun form.

3. Occasionally interference with the pupil's response was caused by some key element in the tester's speech. For example, after hearing the tester say 'Rydyn ni'n gweld gyda'n llygaid', several pupils said 'Rydyn ni'n gweld gyda'n clustiau'.

4. Other items requiring two substitutions presented no difficulty, but an item which required the pupil to make three substitutions often gave rise to incomplete response. 'Mae'r pysgodyn yn nofio yn y dŵr' quite often became 'Mae'r pysgodyn yn y dŵr' or, less frequently, 'Mae'r pysgodyn yn nofio'. The reason for this was not a vocabulary difficulty, as a further question always elicited the rest of the sentence.

5. Items which proved testing to the Welsh-speaking pupils were those using mathematical language, 'mwya' and 'llai', and those using the adjectives 'trwm', 'tenau' and 'sur'.

Of the thirty-five items piloted in this trial twenty-five were selected for the second stage. Nineteen of them had presented little difficulty in the initial test, while six of them had proved difficult, in varying degrees, for seven-year-old Welsh speakers.

Pilot test in Project schools
The oral test administered to a sample of Project schools consisted of the following twenty-five items. The expected responses only are listed below.

> Tri bloc.
> Mae'r gath o dan y gadair.
> Dau gi.
> Het Dadi ydy hon.
> Mae'r babi'n fach.
> Dwy law.

Tri phlentyn.
Mae'r bachgen yn cicio'r bêl.
Rydyn ni'n yfed llaeth.
Rydyn ni'n cysgu yn y nos.
Mae'r dyn yn cerdded.
Rydw i'n gorwedd yn y gwely.
Mae'r bocs mawr yn drwm.
Cot y ferch ydy hon.
Rydyn ni'n clywed gyda'n clustiau.
. . . mwya.
. . . llai na'r ceffyl.
. . . sur.
Mae'r aderyn yn byw mewn nyth.
Mae'r pensil yn denau.
Dillad y bachgen ydy'r rhain.
Mae'r bachgen hwn yn eistedd ar y wal.
Mae'r pysgodyn yn nofio yn y dŵr.
. . . i gyd wedi cwympo lawr.
. . . wedi torri'i gwallt.

The sample of pupils was obtained as follows. In order to obtain a spread of schools across all LEAs participating in the Project, one school was randomly selected from among the schools participating within each LEA, providing a sample of thirteen infant schools or departments which yielded a total of 294 pupils. As the oral test had to be administered individually, it was decided to use a smaller, banded sub-sample from within these schools. The required sample was to consist of three groups, namely, pupils with high achievement in the second language, pupils of average achievement and pupils of low achievement. It was originally intended to select the members of the three groups by selecting three bands from the top, middle and bottom of the results in the listening comprehension test. However as this would have meant waiting until the comprehension tests had been scored before administering the oral test, it would have entailed two tours of Wales to pilot the two tests. In order to save both time and expense, it was decided to ask class teachers to select pupils to represent the three bands. This seemed to work reasonably well in most cases, as when results were compared with the within-school rank order of pupils in the comprehension test, it was found that most of the pupils did in fact fall into the same groups in the comprehension test. However it was sometimes felt that the selection was inappropriate. There was a certain tendency to select from the upper reaches of the average band, while one or two schools had clearly not selected pupils from the lowest band at all. A slight distortion could, it was felt, be tolerated, but any gross deviation from the three-band sample was rectified after testing by referring to the rank order of pupils in the listening comprehension test results, and by re-positioning pupils in the appropriate bands where it was deemed necessary.

out by examining the expected responses and allowing one credit for each substitution supplied by the pupil. Very little credit was given for correct repetition of elements of the tester's speech which appeared in the response. It was not originally planned to award any credits for correct repetition, but in the course of administration it was found that certain elements of repetition did in fact discriminate between pupils being tested, e.g. 'ydy hon', 'rydyn ni', 'rydw i' and 'ydy'r rhain'. It was decided to award one credit for correct repetition of each one of these, so that four of the marks were awarded for correct repetition and forty-six for correct substitution. One word could be worth two credits, one for the use of the word and another for the correct form of the word, e.g. the correct gender or mutation.

The following table summarises the results of scoring the items used in the stage two pilot test both in the three bands of Project pupils and in the sample of Welsh-speakers who had taken part in the first pilot test. Individual scores for the Welsh-speakers were obtained by scoring the same twenty-five items as were used in the second pilot test among Project pupils.

Table 20: Scores obtained in piloting oral test material for infants

	Native speakers Whole range	Project pupils Above average	Average	Below Average
Mean score	38/50	29/50	20/50	12/50
Range of scores	49—9	36—16	26—15	17—6

In order to compare performance in the oral and comprehension tests, the scores of the pupils who appeared in the three-band sample were extracted from the larger sample of pupils who did the listening comprehension test, and the mean scores of the three bands were obtained for both tests. The following table shows the two sets of percentage scores.

Table 21: Scores obtained in piloting oral and comprehension tests in 3 ability bands

	Prawf Llafar Mean score	Gwrando a Deall Mean score
Above average	58%	84%
Average	40%	70%
Below average	24%	47%

The oral test, as was expected, presented a stiffer challenge than the comprehension test.

A facility value for each of the items was obtained by obtaining percentages of correct response to each item. Discrimination values were obtained by comparing item scores of upper and lower bands, although these bands were very narrow in relation to the size of the larger sample from which they were taken. Discrimination values ranged from 0.00 to 0.77. Of the eighteen items which had facility values ranging from thirty-five per cent to seventy-two per cent, fourteen had discrimination values ranging from 0.33 to 0.77. These fourteen items were included in the final test, together with three of the more difficult items, which extended the test for the high achievers. Three of the very easy items were included as practice items. The marking scheme was reviewed, certain additional elements being selected as credit-carrying test elements. The final marking scheme again scored the test out of fifty. Items used in the final test are listed in Appendix B(2) (p.138), together with the facility and discrimination values obtained in the second pilot test. Appendix B(3) (p.139) breaks down response into each credit-carrying test element and shows the facility value obtained for each when the final test was administered in 1973. At this stage no discrimination values were obtained as item selection had been completed.

PRAWF LLAFAR

The oral test was administered to the top infant classes in ten Project schools during the summer of 1973. A total of 149 pupils did the test. The test was scored out of fifty, one credit being given for each test item in the sentence units. Fifteen of the credits were for correct repetition and thirty-five for correct substitution. The table in Appendix B(3) shows the breakdown of the sentence units into test items, the number of correct responses to each item and the facility value obtained by finding the percentage of correct responses to each item.

Difficulties in oral expression

Generally speaking pronunciation difficulties were rare, and accent and information, with a few exceptions, approximated closely to those of native speakers. No account was taken in the marking scheme of pronunciation or intonation. However attention should be drawn to one feature of pronunciation which caused difficulty. Whenever 'mae' occurred followed by the definite article, it was noticed that there was widespread failure to pronounce the 'r' sound in 'mae'r'. It was difficult to know whether the omission was due to a swallowing of the 'r', or whether a habit had been established of ignoring the definite article in this form because it required some effort in pronunciation. It is important that such a habit of speech should not become firmly established, as it is of crucial syntactic importance. A child who has got into the habit of saying 'mae' for 'mae'r' will not be equipped to express in his speech the difference in meaning between, for example, 'Mae'r ci yn yr ardd' and 'Mae ci yn yr ardd'. No account was taken of this feature in marking the oral test, as it was often impossible to decide whether the pupil had in fact pronounced the 'r', but inaudibly, or whether he was consistently ignoring the definite article. It was observed, however, that this particular feature was a fairly good indicator of linguistic background, as pupils with a certain level of Welshness in their family background rarely found any difficulty in using 'mae'r'.

It was suspected that most pupils were quite unaware of the semantic importance of the 'r' sound and that 'mae'r' represented to them one unit of meaning. A chance observation of this feature in a child's written work gave some support to this assumption, and also raised the question of how children of this age learning a second language in this way manage to equate in their minds, if indeed they do so, elements of the first and second languages, when those elements are not easily demonstrable. How do infant learners master the use of the definite article in a case like this, when its formal expression cannot easily be equated in the first and second language? A seven-year-old in one school had written a short description of winter in English, and wanted to write one in Welsh as well. The teacher helped her with some items of vocabulary in her Welsh description. The child then copied both her descriptions on to sheets of paper to be displayed on the wall. She prefaced each one with a title. The English one was entitled 'The Winter' and the Welsh one 'Mae'r gaeaf'. In both cases they were the opening words of her description. It seems clear that 'mae'r' was equated in this child's mind with the English word 'the', although the sentence with which she opened her description, 'Mae'r gaeaf yn oer', was completely correct and gave no clue to any misconception on her part about the meaning of its separate elements.

Most of the sentence units used in this test were based on the basic patterns beginning with 'mae'. Apart from the feature mentioned above, this presented no difficulty. Indeed it was so firmly established that the very weakest pupils proved rather inflexible and began every utterance with the word 'mae', whether appropriate or not. A few other patterns were introduced. The emphatic sentences, 'Côt y ferch ydy hon', 'Dillad y bachgen ydy'r rhain', were on the whole correctly used. Sentences using the first person were a little more difficult. The first person singular form was used more readily than the first person plural. Just over a quarter of the pupils used the past form 'wedi'.

It will be seen from the table in Appendix B (3) that of the substitutions required in this test the nouns as a class presented the least difficulty. Of the dozen nouns required, ten were used correctly by between fifty-three and eighty-three per cent of the pupils. 'Nyth' was used by one third and 'nos' by a quarter of the sample. The prepositions 'ar' and 'yn' presented little difficulty, but 'o dan' was used by only thirty-nine per cent. Of the seven verbs required, 'cysgu', 'cerdded', 'cicio', 'eistedd' and 'nofio' were used by between a half and two-thirds of the sample, but 'yfed' by only one fifth and 'gorwedd' by only seven per cent. The adjective 'mawr' was used by seventy per cent of the pupils, and 'bach', surprisingly, by only fifty-five per cent. 'Trwm' proved much more difficult and was used by only fourteen per cent, while the comparative form 'llai' was used by only seven per cent and proved one of the most difficult items. It will be remembered that this was a difficult item when presented to native-speakers at this age-level and less than half of the Welsh-speaking children succeeded in using it correctly.

The instances of mutation which appear in four items give rise to some interesting observations. The adjective 'mawr' was demanded in the response 'Mae'r bocs mawr yn drwm'. Lexically it was an easy word—seventy per cent used it—but only forty per cent used the form 'mawr', the remaining thirty per cent using the phrase 'bocs fawr'. This suggests that understandable confusion occurs when a common adjective is heard with roughly equal frequency mutated and not mutated in the same kind of pattern—'y tŷ mawr', 'y goeden fawr'. Similarly in another pattern, the adjective following 'yn', while fifty-five per cent were familiar with the word 'bach', only thirty-three per cent said 'Mae'r babi'n fach'. However when the adjective demanded was a difficult item lexically, i.e. 'trwm', all the pupils who were able to use the word mutated it correctly—'yn drwm'. It is possible that that particular item, where learnt, had been heard exclusively in that particular grammatical context, and that the mutated form had been assimilated before the root form. Items such as this suggest that these pupils' assimilation of the second language follows, at least partially, the haphazard, natural kind of assimilation which occurs when children learn their first language. However, with substantially less contact time with the second language available, the process of self-correction is a long drawn out one. The fourth instance of mutation, occuring in the phrase 'cot y ferch—yr eneth', was correctly dealt with by only seven per cent of the pupils, although much larger numbers used the words 'merch' or 'geneth'. The subject of mutation, a major difficulty in the learning of Welsh, prompts one final remark, arising from observation of classroom practice. It was sometimes noticed that infant teachers deliberately avoided using mutated forms, notably after 'dyma'. While their motive in doing this is doubtless a laudable one, namely to simplify the language they are presenting to very young beginners, the wisdom of this practice is nevertheless highly debatable. It must surely implant incorrect speech habits which, at some time or other, will have to be corrected.

One of the most difficult items in this test entailed the expression of the idea of 'all'. Only nine per cent used 'i gyd' or 'pawb' to express this idea, although most of the respondents showed that they had understood the idea conveyed by the picture, many saying 'all' or 'all of them' in English.

The difficulty of the last-mentioned item, and of others of a mathematical nature, suggests that insufficient use has probably been made of directed activities which reinforce mathematical concepts, e.g. size, inclusion, exclusion, and at the same time provide necessary practice in the expression of these concepts in the second language. Similarly one is led to ask why so few children could find a word to express the idea of drinking, moreover in the context of children drinking milk, when this activity must be a ritual part of every infant school day. Actions which recur as often as this should be seized upon in a bilingual programme and used as a basis for the incidental use of the second language which is such an important aid both to understanding and expression. The small numbers of pupils who used the verb 'gorwedd' suggest that greater use could be made of the second language in music and movement or action stories to teach the use of verbs of this nature.

Test scores
Prawf Llafar, the oral test, proved to be rather more difficult than *Prawf Gwrando a Deall,* the listening comprehension test. This is not surprising since the skill of understanding is a lower-level one than that of oral expression. The scores obtained out of fifty in both tests reflect the different levels of difficulty of the two tests. In the oral test the range of scores was 0-46 and the mean score was 23. Within this group mean scores were calculated for those pupils who had done both oral and comprehension tests. The resulting group of 143 pupils had a mean score of 25 in the oral test and 33 in the comprehension test. The mean score in *Prawf Gwrando a Deall* for the whole group of 704 pupils was 28, i.e. five points lower than that of the smaller group. As there is a clear relationship between scores in the two tests it is fair to assume that if all the pupils could have done the oral test their mean score would probably have been several points lower than twenty-five out of fifty.

Variables affecting performance
The length of time for which pupils had followed the Project was the first variable examined in relation to the oral test. The following table summarises results in the four categories of this variable.

Table 22: Prawf Llafar *results within four categories*

Length of time pupils had followed Project	No. of scores	Mean score	Standard deviation
1. 3 yrs. and over	8	20.87	10.55
2. 2 yrs. to 2 yrs. 11 mths.	64	26.37	9.65
3. 1 yr. to 1 yr. 11 mths.	75	24.39	10.09
4. Less than 1 yr.	2	17.00	14.00

In the relatively small sample doing this test the number of pupils falling into the two extreme categories was negligible, so that the chi-square tests took account of the two main categories only. The distribution of scores, using pupils in the second and third categories only, i.e. those who had followed the Project for just under three years and those who had followed the Project for just under two years, revealed no significant difference between the two groups (v. *Table 23* below). So in oral expression as well as in levels of comprehension it appears that roughly the same level of attainment is reached whether the Project is implemented for two or three years in the infant schools. One is prompted to wonder why, if this level of attainment can be reached in two years, a third year does not extend the pupils still further.

Results were next examined in relation to the amount of time devoted to Project work in the school day. It so happened that not one of the small number of schools where the time devoted to Project work was judged to be clearly insufficient appeared in the sample for the oral test. It has previously been seen that there was little difference between the performance of the remaining two categories in the *Prawf Gwrando a Deall*. As only schools from these two categories appeared in the smaller sample, it is only a reflection of the earlier result that this factor proved not to be significant in the oral test results either. Had one or more of the schools devoting inadequate time to the Project appeared in the sample, the level of their scores, it can be fairly safely predicted, would doubtless have brought about a different result.

When the factors of sex, and socio-economic background were examined in relation to the oral test scores, neither factor was found to affect performance in this test. The results parallel those obtained from examining *Prawf Gwrando a Deall* scores in relation to these two factors.

Of all the background factors examined, only one proved to have a significant influence on performance in the oral test, namely the linguistic background of the school. The higher the level of Welshness present in the school and its neighbourhood, the more likely were the pupils to achieve high oral test scores. Conversely, in schools in highly anglicised areas, where pupils had little or no contact with Welsh outside school, it was more difficult to achieve high scores in the oral test. It is interesting to note that this factor did not have any apparent effect on the more passive skill of comprehension, but it does appear to influence oral attainment.

The following table summarises the results of chi-square tests using oral test scores in relation to one other variable. The results should be interpreted in the light of remarks made in the preceding paragraphs. Contingency tables from which chi-square values were obtained are reproduced in Appendix D (p.152).

Table 23: Values of chi-square obtained from relating 5 variables to scores in Prawf Llafar

Variable	Value of chi-square	d.f.	Level of significance
Sex	5.82	2	Not significant
Socio-economic background	9.96	8	Not significant
Linguistic background of school	15.55	4	0.005
Time following Project	0.43	2	Not significant (2 categories only)
Time devoted to Project	5.54	2	Not significant (2 categories only)

The oral test scores correlated much more highly with those of the listening comprehension test than with any of the NFER tests given. The following table summarises the results of chi-square tests using oral test scores in relation to scores in three other tests.

Table 24: Values of chi-square obtained from relating scores in Prawf Llafar *to scores in 3 other tests*

Variable	Value of chi-square	d.f.	Level of significance
Gwrando a Deall	59.40	4	0.001
Picture Test A	7.55	4	Not significant
Reading Test BD	9.60	4	0.05

Performance in the Welsh oral test showed some correlation with performance in the test of English reading, but none with the non-verbal ability test, *Picture Test A*. The converse was true of performance in the Welsh comprehension test.

CONSTRUCTING A WELSH TEST FOR JUNIORS

The task of constructing a second-language test for the second-year junior pupils was beset with certain difficulties. Firstly it was observed that the operation of the Project in the junior schools was such that it was difficult, if not impossible, to find any common core of subject-matter studied through the medium of the second language. The freedom which this Project allowed its teachers to choose or create their own study-schemes, either from materials prepared or suggested by the Project team or from some other source, meant that there was no hope of basing test items on any common contextual ground, or of testing language usage within a defined lexical framework. There had been, of course, the same freedom of approach allowed in the infant schools. A framework had ·been provided by the teachers' handbook,[2] but within this, considerable latitude was enjoyed by teachers to choose the activities they wished to pursue. Nevertheless observation of the work done over the range of infant schools suggested that a common core of what is regarded as essential infant-school experience was built into the work of the second-language sessions in most infant schools. This resulted in a considerable overlap of experience from school to school. Furthermore the listening books prepared by the Project team and used by most schools also helped to build a linguistic framework, both lexical and syntactic. In creating tests, therefore, one could be fairly confident of working within an area most of which would have been covered by the infant schools being tested.

In the junior schools departures were made in many different directions. The lack of uniformity of subject-matter studied made it difficult to find a common core of vocabulary on which to base the tests. Furthermore the projected reading scheme mentioned in the statement of aims [2] was not developed. Such a scheme, supplemented by a series of readers, might have fulfilled in the junior schools a role parallel to that played by the listening books in the infant schools. Under the circumstances the basis of test content had to be as follows. As far as syntax was concerned, note was taken of the instructions circulated to junior schools in duplicated material, both in separate leaflets and in the original draft of the volume *Dyn wrth ei waith*.[6] As far as vocabulary was concerned, care was taken to avoid, as far as possible, any very specialised vocabulary, and to draw only on what could reasonably be regarded as a basic vocabulary.

The lack of a reading scheme raised another difficulty too with regard to test strategy. The fact that it had not proved possible to develop such a scheme meant that the Project schools had not followed any common policy with regard to the development of reading skill in Welsh. Could, therefore, second-language reading ability be taken for granted when constructing tests? Or should this area of language skills be completely ignored and the testing restricted once again, as it had been at infant level, to aural-oral skills? Consultation with the Project officers and teachers, and observation of children's work at this age-level all pointed to the fact that both reading and writing skills were being used in the junior schools. Furthermore there would be considerable difficulties in constructing an adequate test consisting only of aural-oral components in a comparatively short time. Even at infant level the visual material used had had to be fairly complex. The increased complexity of language to be tested at junior level would correspondingly increase the complexity of the visual material needed. The quality and amount of visual material required would make it very expensive in financial terms, but more importantly it would require extensive piloting of pictures and here the time factor was crucial. Junior tests were being prepared by the Project research officer during the same year as the final testing was being carried out in the infant schools. There was less time available for the preparation of junior tests than there had been for the preparation of infant tests.

The final decision made was to use a paper-and-pencil test, assuming reading skill, but including, in the initial piloting at least, some pictorial material, coupled with reading matter, in order to test this assumption, and attempt to ascertain whether reading skill had in fact been established to a level which would enable pupils to cope with this kind of test. The test administered to the junior classes would be a group test, parallelling the listening comprehension group test administered to infant classes. In addition to this an oral test would be constructed. The nature of this will be described in a later section. In constructing the paper-and-pencil group test considerable use was made of Welsh test items created or collected by members of the Schools Council Project on Attitudes to Welsh and English in the schools of Wales.[7] These items had already been piloted, some on second-language pupils and some on first-language pupils in junior schools.

Initial pilot test
It was decided to carry out the piloting in two stages. In the initial stage, ten questions, containing items ranging over a wide range of facility, were tried out in the second-year junior classes of four Project schools. The questions fell into two categories. Four of them tested reading comprehension, most of the items being of the multiple-choice variety. The remaining six questions tested various features of syntax, vocabulary and language usage, three of these

also being of the multiple-choice variety. Eighty-three items were included in this first trial, which was carried out by the research officer. The schools used, although only four in number, covered a wide range of pupil ability and socio-economic background, and also showed some variety in modes of Project implementation. The following list describes what the pupil was required to do in each question.

Reading comprehension
A. From four pictures select the one corresponding to a printed sentence.
B. From four printed sentences select the one which describes a picture.
C. Read a passage of prose and answer questions

and D. to test understanding of the passage.

Language use
A. Re-arrange scrambled sentences.
B. Fill in blanks in sentences by choosing one of four responses—a test of grammatical features.
C. Supply plural forms of nouns.
D. Supply singular forms of nouns.
E. Choose the correct answer to a question out of four listed responses—a test of verb forms.
F. Read a complete English sentence, then the corresponding Welsh sentence which contains a blank space, and fill in the missing word by choosing one of four responses—a test of vocabulary.

After these questions had been scored, an average score was calculated for each question within classes. This provided a range of facility values for each question, i.e. set of items. The reading comprehension questions A and B proved to be by far the easiest, with class averages ranging from seventy to eighty per cent. This seemed to support the assumption that reading skill had been sufficiently well established to enable most of the pupils to cope with a test which involved reading. It was decided that these two questions were not testing enough and they were omitted from the second stage of the pilot testing. It was decided that language use question E should be extended to include more items of a similar nature.

Second stage pilot test
After these initial amendments had been carried out, the test, now consisting of seventy items, was administered in three further

schools. The three largest schools in the remaining pool were chosen. By the time the material was ready for the second stage of piloting, the final stage of infant-school testing was about to begin. As this was to occupy the research officer until the end of the school year, the head teachers of these schools were approached, and they agreed to take charge of pilot test administration during the second stage, and to return the completed scripts to the research officer for scoring.

After all scripts had been scored and results despatched to the schools which had taken part in the pilot testing, facility values were obtained for each of the items. In the light of these it was decided to discard language usage question F, which had proved the most difficult question overall. It was felt that the nature of the items, which involved a process of translation to which the pupils were not accustomed, made them unsuitable for these pupils. Other minor adjustments were made. Some items were omitted because they were too easy, others because they were too difficult, and a few because they were unsatisfactory for some other reason.

It had been hoped to produce a final version of the test consisting of fifty items, and divided into two roughly equal parts. It proved possible to do this and the test was printed in two parts, entitled *Prawf Cymraeg A* and *Prawf Cymraeg B*. Each part contained twenty-five items, seven of them being comprehension questions based on a prose passage and the remaining eighteen items testing various features of language usage. The facility values of the items included (i.e. percentage of correct response in the pilot test) ranged from 0.08 to 0.81. The distribution of items over this range was as follows:

> 6 items below 0.20
> 8 items between 0.21 and 0.30
> 7 items between 0.31 and 0.40
> 8 items between 0.41 and 0.50
> 8 items between 0.51 and 0.60
> 8 items between 0.61 and 0.70
> 4 items between 0.71 and 0.80
> 1 item between 0.81 and 1.00

The final version of the test is printed in Appendix B (4) (p.140).

PRAWF CYMRAEG

The Welsh group test for juniors was administered to second-year classes in twenty Project schools at the end of the Easter term in 1974. The total number of pupils who sat the test was 475. Only pupils who had followed the Project programme for the whole time they had been in the junior school and for at least one school year in the infant school were included in the group whose scores were used in the subsequent analysis. When others who did not satisfy these criteria were omitted, the number of scores remaining was 427.

The test which consisted of fifty items was scored out of fifty. The mean score for the whole group was 15.34 and the scores ranged from two to forty-four. The mean score and distribution of scores indicated that the test was a difficult one for this group of pupils. It had been intended to create as testing an instrument as possible, one which would stretch the highest achievers, while being at the same time a reasonably discriminatory instrument for use with the whole range of pupils being tested. In the final administration, the test did present a stiff challenge to the high achievers, so that some idea of the ceiling of attainment can be given. However the high proportion of difficult items included meant that the lower achievers bunched together at the lower end of the scoring range. The reason for the unexpected behaviour of the test when administered to the whole range of Project schools probably lies in the different administrative procedures used in the second stage pilot test in 1973 and the final test in 1974. In the previous section of this report, the distribution of the items selected over a facility range of 0.08 to 0.81 was given. In the table below the same fifty items are grouped within categories over the facility range which occurred in the final pilot test.

Table 25: Facility values of items in Prawf Cymraeg *in final test and in pilot test administration.*

Facility values	No. of items in final testing	No. of items in pilot testing
Below 0.20	13	6
0.21 to 0.30	17	8
0.31 to 0.40	12	7
0.41 to 0.50	2	8
0.51 to 0.60	5	8
0.61 to 0.70	0	8
0.71 to 0.80	1	4
0.81 to 1.00	0	1

A comparison of the two distributions shows that the same

selection of items proved much more difficult in the Project-administered test administration than in the partly school-administered pilot test. Another factor which might have contributed partially to the discrepancy was the possibility that the seven schools used in the pilot testing did not accurately reflect the range of attainment in the twenty schools available in 1974. This result was disappointing because it meant that the test was a less effective instrument than had been hoped. Nevertheless a good deal of information can be extracted from an examination of the pupils' performance.

Facility levels

The impression gained while administering and scoring the test was that the pupils were on the whole able to read for understanding at a simple level in their second language, but that discrimination between most of the grammatical features appearing in the test was beyond the powers of the majority. For example, about half the pupils were able to select the correct answer to the question 'Faint o'r gloch ydy hi?' when, in order to score, the pupil had to read for meaning only. But only about a fifth of the pupils could select the correct verb form required to answer the question 'Oeddech chi'n canu yn y côr?' It was not surprising, of course, that the complexities of using the appropriate verb forms for affirmative and negative replies should cause difficulties, and the selection of the verb forms 'ydyn', 'oedden' and 'ie' proved to be among the most difficult items in the test.

However it would not be true to say that all or even most of the items which involved comprehension only were easier than those dealing with grammar. The easiest item of all was the selection of 'Oes' in answer to the question 'Oes arian gyda chi?' This was correctly selected by almost three-quarters of the pupils. The selection of 'ydy' to complete the question 'Pwy—e?' was correctly made by forty-three per cent. All the other items involving verb forms proved more difficult than the two just mentioned, and their facility values ranged from 0.39 to 0.19. Thirty-nine per cent correctly selected 'Nac ydw' to answer the question 'Dydych chi ddim wedi gweld Sioned?' About one third selected 'Do' and 'Naddo' where appropriate. Only about a quarter could select the appropriate negative forms 'Doedd e' and 'Dydw i'. 'Oeddwn', 'oeddech' and 'ydyn' were the most difficult items testing verb forms.

Another type of question, which entailed writing either the singular or the plural form of nouns, also contained items varying widely in facility. Well over half the pupils could supply the singular forms 'afon' and 'aderyn' and the plural form 'coed'. About a third knew the plurals 'traed' and 'llygaid', but considerably less could supply 'tai' and 'dynion' or give the singular forms of 'lloriau', 'defaid' and 'ieir'.

The question which required pupils to write out a series of scrambled sentences correctly proved to be a difficult one. The easiest items in this series were correctly unscrambled by about one-third of the pupils while the four most difficult were unscrambled by between four and sixteen per cent only.

The facility values of all the test items, as obtained in the final test administration, are given in Appendix B (4) (p.140).

It must be remembered that practice in second-language use is still carried on to a very large extent orally at this stage in the primary school, and that the use of a paper-and-pencil test might be said not to reflect adequately a pupil's powers in dealing with some features of language use. Although it had been established that reading, both for pleasure and for information, and writing for the purpose of recording, were common practice at this level in the junior schools many teachers pointed out that formal reading and writing did not form part of the second-language programme and expressed fears that the pupils would not perform well because they had not been formally trained in these skills. However account had been taken of this situation in constructing the test. Most of the items were of the multiple-choice variety, so the pupils were required to write only in a small number of items. When they were, they were not penalised for misspellings. For example 'tie' and 'tried' were accepted as correct plural forms of 'tŷ' and 'troed', and 'davad' and 'aderin' were judged equally acceptable singular forms. In the case of the selection of verb forms such as 'ydyn' or 'oeddwn', it might be argued that the visual discrimination between, say, 'ydy' and 'ydyn' on the printed page would prove an obstacle to a pupil who might be able to use them correctly in speech. However this was not borne out by the sample of pupils who did the oral test. Very few of these, as will be shown in a later section, could use the reply form 'ydyn' in the oral test unit in which this was required, so it would seem that their performance in the paper-and-pencil test reflected in some instances at least, their oral use of language.

For one group of pupils, however, the test probably did not adequately reflect their powers of comprehension of the spoken word. This group consisted of the very poor readers. There were some in whom reading skill had not yet been firmly established in the first language. They were fortunately not very numerous, but their handicap made it almost impossible for them to extract meaning from the test booklets.

One final observation can be made which throws some light on the facility level of the test. Among the pupils who took this test, it was possible to identify three who may be regarded as native speakers of Welsh. Two of them were girls whose parents spoke Welsh, who had followed the Project programme from early in their infant schools and who also made use of Welsh in certain circumstances outside school. The third was a boy who had been transferred from a Welsh stream to a Project class at the beginning of the term in which the test was administered. Although he took the test, he was not included in the group whose scores were used in the analysis. The scores, out of fifty, which these three pupils gained were as follows: 33, 37 and 34. All three were pupils in different schools and in different counties. Although comment about such a small number must be guarded, the similarity of their scores makes an interesting comparison with the average score levels of the whole range of Project pupils. In classes where the Project was being satisfactorily implemented, roughly five per cent of the pupils reached a level of attainment in this test comparable to that reached by the three pupils mentioned above.

Project implementation

The first variable examined in relation to the test was that relating to the implementation of the Project in each school, or, in each class within a school. When this factor was discussed with members of the Project team, it was felt that this could best be considered as one factor consisting of several components. Those components were—

> the attitude of the head teacher,
> the attitude of members of staff responsible for the Project programme,
> the amount of time devoted to the Project programme in the school day,
> the teachers' preparation of suitable materials, careful presentation of new language patterns, and marrying of content with the pupils' linguistic competence,
> the availability of bilingual staff.

When these components were kept in mind, it was relatively easy to group classes into two categories, those where the Project was being implemented satisfactorily and those where it was not. It will be noted that, in considering the junior schools, the amount of time devoted to the Project was not taken as the key factor as it had been in the infant schools. At both infant and junior levels the Project recommended that either the afternoon session or its equivalent in time should be devoted to work through the medium of Welsh. Compliance with this request was not nearly as widespread in the junior schools as it had been in the infant schools. Nevertheless it was not felt that this factor alone reflected successful or unsuccessful implementation. For example, one school had decided to allocate one hour a day to the Project programme. This school adhered scrupulously to this allocation, work was conscientiously prepared and imaginatively presented, it was fully supported by the head teacher, who ensured that incidental use was made of Welsh in the life of the school and who encouraged extra-curricular activities in Welsh. This school was felt to be implementing the Project satisfactorily, as the curtailment of time was compensated for by the fact that all the other criteria were completely fulfilled. On the other hand there were examples of schools where nominally at least, sufficient time was allocated, but where other factors militated against success.

The influence of Project implementation on second-language attainment could be perceived first of all in the variation in class averages in the test. These ranged from 8.23 to 19.11. There were sometimes observable differences between classes within schools. When all pupils had been allocated to one or other of the two categories of Project implementation, it was found that these categories were almost equal in size. One half of the Project pupils, therefore, were following the Project programme under conditions judged to be less than satisfactory. The following table summarises test results within the two categories of Project implementation.

Table 26: Results in Prawf Cymraeg *within two categories of Project implementation*

Project implementation	No. of pupils	Mean score	Range of scores	Standard deviation
Satisfactory	215	16.87	3—44	7.99
Not satisfactory	212	13.34	2—33	5.57

In the junior schools, as in the infant schools, lower attainment in

102

the second language is associated with unsatisfactory conditions for implementing the Project. However the number of infant pupils affected by adverse conditions of implementation was very much smaller than the number of juniors handicapped in this way. The following table shows the breakdown of numbers into three bands of attainment in *Prawf Cymraeg* within the two categories.

Table 27: Contingency table and value of chi-square obtained from relating two categories of Project implementation to attainment in Prawf Cymraeg

| Attainment | Project implementation | |
	Not satisfactory	Satisfactory
Low	84	67
Average	106	80
High	22	68
Chi-square = 29.04		
Significant at level of 0.001	d.f. = 2	

The value of chi-square in the above table denotes the high level of significance of this factor in second-language attainment.

Pupil variables
From this point the influence of pupil variables was examined within the two categories of Project implementation and not within the group as a whole. The more useful examination is the one carried out among pupils following the Project programme under satisfactory conditions, but the behaviour of both groups will be described because interesting differences between them occur.

The pupils' scores were examined in relation to three pupil variables, sex, socio-economic background and linguistic background. Pupils were placed in one of four categories of linguistic background. The following table shows the number of pupils within each category.

Table 28: Numbers of pupils in four categories of linguistic background in second-year junior classes

Category	Nature of category	No. of pupils
0	Neither parent speaking Welsh	286
1	Father speaking Welsh, but not mother	54
2	Mother speaking Welsh, but not father	45
3	Both parents speaking Welsh	42

Of the 427 pupils tested, ten per cent had two Welsh-speaking parents, about a quarter of the remainder had at least one Welsh-speaking parent, and the rest had two English-speaking parents.

The following tables shows the chi-square values obtained from relating attainment scores in *Prawf Cymraeg* and three pupil variables, within the category in which the Project was implemented satisfactorily. Contingency tables from which chi-square values were obtained are reproduced in Appendix D (p.152).

Table 29: Values of chi-square obtained from relating scores in Prawf Cymraeg *to three pupil variables, using pupils following the Project programme under satisfactory conditions*

Variable	Value of chi-square	d.f.	Level of significance
Sex	4.05	2	Not significant
Socio-economic background	20.79	8	0.01
Linguistic background	4.86	6	Not significant

Where the Project was implemented satisfactorily, neither the pupil's sex nor linguistic background had a significant effect on attainment, but socio-economic background did prove significant, the highest socio-economic group tending to gain high scores, while the lowest group tended to gain low scores.

The next table shows the chi-square values obtained from relating attainment scores in *Prawf Cymraeg* to the same three pupil variables within the category in which the Project was not judged to be implemented satisfactorily.

Table 30: Values of chi-square obtained from relating scores in Prawf Cymraeg *to three pupil variables, using pupils following the Project programme under unsatisfactory conditions*

Variable	Value of chi-square	d.f.	Level of significance
Sex	5.33	2	Not significant
Socio-economic background	14.62	8	Not significant
Linguistic background	23.52	6	0.001

In this category the effects of socio-economic background and linguistic background are reversed. Here linguistic background is highly significant, whereas where the Project was better implemented it was not. This suggests that effective presentation of a second language in school can allow pupils whose parents speak English only to reach levels of attainment comparable to those achieved by pupils with the initial advantage of a more Welsh background. However socio-economic background seems to have a significant effect only when instruction is more effective, suggesting that the socially advantaged can double their advantage when the programme is effective but when it is less effective they have no more of a headstart than anyone else.

Within the sample of eight schools in which NFER tests were administered to the second-year junior classes, it was possible to relate the pupils' performance in *Prawf Cymraeg* to their performance in the battery of NFER tests. The chi-square values obtained are shown in the table below.

Table 31: *Values of chi-square obtained from relating scores in* Prawf Cymraeg *to scores in five NFER tests*

Test	Value of chi-square	d.f.	Level of significance
Reading BD	26.24	4	0.001
Mathematics B	18.28	4	0.01
English Progress B2	30.66	4	0.001
Non-Verbal BD	21.44	4	0.001
Verbal BC	26.16	4	0.001

The Welsh test results correlated highly with those in all five other tests, although the level of significance was not as high in the case of the mathematics test as it was for the other four tests. The results shown in table 31 were obtained from using scores of pupils in the category of satisfactory Project implementation.

It must be concluded that, although socio-economic background has some influence on pupil performance in the Welsh test, the most powerful factor is undoubtedly the mode of Project implementation prevailing in the school or in the classroom.

What inhibits successful implementation

A brief outline of the main components of successful implementation of the bilingual education Project has been given earlier in this section. Since as much as half the Project population in the second-year junior age-group in 1974 was felt not to be following the programme under satisfactory conditions, it is important to try to ascertain what are the inhibitors which hamper the implementation of such a programme in the junior schools. The availability of enough bilingual teachers to carry on the Project programme throughout the school is a basic essential. Ideally this means a bilingual teacher in every class which follows the bilingual programme. Where this is impossible the employment of a specialist teacher can be very successful, although if the specialist's time is shared among too many classes this will curtail the contact time of each class with the second language. Where a specialist is employed, it is preferable that he or she should be a full-time member of the school staff and thus able to contribute to the bilingualism of the school in extra-curricular activities.

Favourable attitudes towards bilingual education on the part of both head and class teachers are also important. Unfavourable attitudes often stem from sincere doubt either about the feasibility of such a programme or about its educational effects. It is to be hoped that the information gathered in the course of the Project's operation will be helpful in allowing schools to make a more informed judgment in the future about the possibilities of implementing a programme of bilingual education in their particular circumstances.

Even given the basic requirements of bilingual competence and willingness to undertake the programme, all teachers undertaking such work need considerable support and training in the techniques involved in presenting a second language to young pupils and using it as a medium of instruction while pupils are still in the process of learning the language. Perhaps one reason for the fact that the junior programme seemed more difficult to implement than the infant programme was that by the time the Project was becoming established in the junior schools, the Project's budget was becoming strained and less in-service training was being provided. Some teachers commented that they had had to rely mainly on the advice of teachers in classes below theirs in facing the task of implementing the Project, and had initially felt unconfident and insecure about carrying it out. Many gained confidence as they became more familiar with the situation, but much depended on the individual's self-confidence and tenacity. It is felt that information and an opportunity for discussion of the underlying principles of such a programme, as well as more specific advice about methodology should be available to all teachers before they undertake a programme of bilingual education.

In schools which have traditionally carried on their corporate life and daily routine through the medium of English only, it is often difficult, even where it is quite possible, to change established habits and learn to use a second language as part of the currency of everyday talk, incidentally in the classroom, in the school hall and corridors, in the playground and the school bus. Yet the everyday routine presents innumerable opportunities of using Welsh in situations which are real and meaningful to the children. Pupils who never hear their teachers exchange small talk or pass on information in Welsh are deprived of an awareness of the utility of the language they are learning, and also of the opportunity of listening to and understanding adults speaking together in that language. It is hard to break old habits, particularly habits of language use, but the incidental use of Welsh is of immeasurable value in bringing the language alive to pupils who may rarely, if ever, have contact with it in their families.

One difficulty faced by junior teachers is the wide range of competence in the use of the second language among the pupils who enter the junior schools. While this is true of other areas of the curriculum too, it does present an added difficulty to a teacher who is new to the task of implementing a bilingual programme. It is felt that the very slow language learners should be identified during their last year in the infant school, and an attempt be made to provide short remedial programmes for them, both before they leave the infant school and after they reach the junior school. This might help to strengthen the language skills of those who have been reaching the junior schools unable to pursue a bilingual programme at the same level as the majority of the pupils.

Finally it is felt that the absence of a uniform policy with regard to introducing reading and writing has been a handicap in some cases. The provision of a reading scheme would probably aid the implementation of the Project by strengthening the basic language skills of the pupils. However this should be treated as a tool rather than as an end in itself. Care should be taken to avoid turning the Project programme into a purely language programme. Language skills should be strengthened in order to facilitate the use of the language as a medium through which to explore the world which is opening out before the junior school child.

AN ORAL TEST FOR JUNIORS

The short oral test based on pairs of pictures had proved to be a satisfactory instrument for use with the seven-year-old pupils. Its length, ease of administration and discriminatory power had made it a useful measure. However it was felt that something more should be attempted with the older pupils, which would reflect oral proficiency on a broader front than had been possible with the younger children. To do this, a rather different testing strategy was devised.

Firstly it was accepted that the 'test' must be a much longer one and that substantially more time would have to be spent with each individual pupil tested. A variety of units would be included, so as to break down the period of time and avoid boredom and fatigue. The paired pictures format would be used again for part of the test, but other visual and auditory stimuli would also be used. The decision to lengthen considerably the time spent with each pupil meant that the number of pupils tested would have to be greatly reduced. Furthermore one had to decide whether to use only a few schools, testing each pupil in the year-group, or to visit a larger number of schools, testing only a sample of pupils in each school. It was decided to follow the latter course and ten of the twenty available junior schools were visited, and a small number of pupils was interviewed in each school. The pupils tested were chosen to represent three bands of language ability—above average, average and below average. The choice of pupils was made in consultation with the head and class teachers, taking into account, wherever possible, any measures of second-language ability which had previously been administered.

It was accepted that not all units of the test would be easily scoreable. While some units contained items of a 'closed' nature, expecting a certain response and therefore easily scoreable, other units permitted a more open-ended response. The latter kind, while they could not be scored as the others could, would furnish a useful description of features of oral response, and could also be used with a small sample of native speakers of the same age-groups as a basis for comparing features of their language with those of the Project pupils.

It was decided to use the test given to the infants as the first unit of the test for the second-year junior pupils. The purpose of this was to measure the difference between scores of infants and juniors. The whole test consisted of seven units. Each unit will now be described and an account given of levels of performance in each unit. In units 1 to 3 reference will be made to scoring levels. In units 4 to 7, where scoring was not appropriate, a descriptive account will be given of pupil performance, using numerous examples of transcribed material to illustrate the different levels of performance. The items contained in unit 1 can be seen in Appendix B(3) (p.139) and those in units 2, 3 and 7 can be seen in Appendix B(5) (p.148). As the visual material used in the other unit is difficult to reproduce, a description of what was required in each unit will be given in the text below.

Unit 1

This consisted of the seventeen items used in the infants' oral test. The chief interest of this unit lay in the comparison of the scores of the junior pupils with those of the infants. The following table shows the mean scores and range of scores of the two main categories of infants tested in 1973 and the three bands of second-year junior pupils tested in 1974.

Table 32: Scores out of 50 obtained by infant and junior pupils in oral test unit 1

	No. of pupils	Mean score	Range of scores
Top infants in 3rd Project year	64	26.37	6—47
Top infants in 2nd Project year	75	24.39	2—46
Juniors of high ability	14	40.00	37—49
Juniors of average ability	12	32.00	30—36
Juniors of low ability	14	22.50	1—29

The mean scores show that the average and high-ability junior pupils attained score levels substantially superior to the average scores of the infants, but that the low-ability junior pupils scored slightly less than the average score for the whole range of infants. However it is true to say that on the whole the junior pupils of all ability levels scored higher than the younger pupils of corresponding ability. It did not prove to be necessarily true that all pupils had increased their language competence as reflected in this test unit. The pupils tested in the junior schools were not the same pupils as those who had been tested the previous year. However in two junior schools it was possible to test a few pupils who had taken part in the piloting of items for unit 1 of the oral test two years previously. One of these schools was judged not to be implementing the Project satisfactorily, and in this school each of the pupils tested had a lower score at the age of nine than he or she had obtained at the age of seven. This bears out the judgement of field workers, namely that where the junior school approach to Project implementation is less than satisfactory, the pupils' oral skills in the second language do not simply remain at the level reached in infant school, but are actually eroded. The other school in which it was possible to make this comparison was one where Project implementation was judged to be fully satisfactory. In this case both pupils who had been tested at the age of seven increased their scores by the age of nine.

Unit 2

This unit (v. Appendix B(5) p.148) contained a further eight items similar in format to those of unit 1. These items had proved much too difficult for the seven-year-old Project pupils, and had caused some difficulty among seven-year-old native speakers. When piloted on a small sample of nine-year-old native speakers, these items caused little difficulty. When administered to the nine-year-old Project pupils they proved to be much more difficult than the items in unit 1, most of which tested the description of action or position rather than of attributes. The unit was scored out of fifteen. The average scores and range of scores in each band of pupils tested is shown in the following table.

Table 33: Scores out of 15 obtained by junior pupils in oral test unit 2

Band	No. of pupils	Mean score	Range of scores
High-ability pupils	14	3.43	1—7
Average-ability pupils	12	2.00	1—4
Low-ability pupils	14	0.64	0—3

Unit 3

This unit (v. Appendix B(5)) used pictures and a question-and-answer technique to elicit affirmative and negative replies in the singular and plural of verb forms in the present tense. Each question was based on a black-and-white drawing. A few practice items were used to train the children in the mode of response required. The average and above-average bands responded quite well in these items. The main weaknesses of these two bands were the omission if the 'r' sound in 'mae'r', their complete failure to use the plural form 'ydyn', a failure to mutate correctly in 'i gysgu', and the use of 'dim rhywun' and 'dim rhywbeth' instead of 'neb' and 'dim byd'. The below-average band showed less flexibility in the use of the various verb forms, incorrectly used the form 'ydw' and found negative forms difficult to handle. The very weakest pupils tested sometimes found it impossible to hold the sound of the complete sentence, and the reply either tailed off before the end or was compressed into a kind of shorthand. The following table shows the scores gained by the three bands in this unit.

Table 34: Scores out of 20 obtained by junior pupils in oral test unit 3

Band	No. of pupils	Mean score	Range of scores
High-ability pupils	14	11	6—17
Average-ability pupils	12	10	5—14
Low-ability pupils	14	7	2—14

Performance in scored units

Marks obtained in the first three units were summed to obtain a mark for each individual out of a possible total of eighty-five. The following table shows the scores thus obtained in the ability bands.

Table 35: Scores out of 85 obtained by junior pupils in oral test units 1, 2 and 3

Band	No. of pupils	Mean score	Range of scores
High-ability pupils	14	54	49—73
Average-ability pupils	12	44	38—52
low-ability pupils	14	30	4—45

The scores of the pupils included in these three bands were compared with the scores they had obtained in the group test, *Prawf Cymraeg*. Both sets of scores are given as percentages in the table below.

Table 36: Percentage scores obtained by juniors in 3 units of Prawf Llafar *and in* Prawf Cymraeg

Band	No. of Pupils	Mean score in *Prawf Llafar*	Mean score in *Prawf Cymraeg*
High-ability pupils	14	64%	56%
Average-ability pupils	12	52%	38%
Low-ability pupils	14	35%	26%

Unit 4

This unit contained a selection of pictures from magazines showing people, usually children, in everyday circumstances or performing common actions, each one being used to elicit a short reply about what the people were doing. The chief interest of this unit lay in testing the use of common vocabulary arising in situations likely to be familiar or interesting to a child. The pictures used could not be reproduced in the appendix, but an example of response will explain the nature of this unit. The following descriptions of the fourteen pictures used were given by one of the girls in the high-ability band. Neither of this pupil's parents spoke Welsh. The words in brackets were not spoken by the child but have been inserted to explain the nature of the item.

> Mae'r bobl yn edrych ar y plant yn nofio yn y dŵr.
> Mae'r plant yn eistedd i lawr yn yr haul. Mae bechgyn yn rhoi dŵr ar y . . . (lawnt).
> Mae'r dyn hwn yn mynd i paentio ar y wal.
> Maen nhw yn mynd yn yr awyren troi y world (o gwmpas y byd).
> Mae'r plant yn y parti.
> Mae'r eneth fach yn rhoi dillad yn y . . . (peiriant golchi).
> Mae'r wraig o dan y gwallt i wneud y gwallt yn sych.
> Mae'r eneth yn edrych i fyny i'r awyr. Mae hi yn y cwch.
> Maen nhw yn mynd ar y môr yn y cwch.
> Maen nhw yn sglefrio ar y dŵr.
> Mae hi yn rhoi papur ar y wal.
> Maen nhw yn bwyta ar y cwch.
> Mae'r dyn hwn yn edrych ar y penguins.
> Maen nhw yn cael rope yn y dwylo ac yn . . . beth ydy pulling? . . . bocs mawr.

On the whole this pupil had little difficulty in expressing herself and responded fluently. However although she could describe people water-skiing, she could not use the verb 'tynnu' and avoided using the verb 'gorwedd'. The average pupils had surprising difficulty in finding words to express the verbs 'put', 'pull', 'lie' and 'dry' and usually inserted these and other words in English. The weakest pupils used the most English words, and often began sentences with words like 'Mae'r plant yn . . .' or 'Mae'r dyn yn . . .' and finished them off in English.

Although no measurements of time were made, time taken to respond was also a discriminatory feature in this and later units. The below-average pupils showed hesitancy in replying and their words were widely spaced out, whereas the best pupils spoke fluently and at a speed comparable to that of native speakers.

Unit 5
This unit contained three pictures each displaying some unusual feature. The children were asked to say what they thought was funny or odd about each picture. The three items of this unit were administered to a sample of twelve native speakers of Welsh in the same age-group, as well as to the three bands of Project pupils. Sample responses to each picture drawn from each of the four groups are given below.

Picture 1, an advertisement for Credit Agricole, showed a house with a smiling face. Here are some of the responses.

> Native speakers.
>> Mae gwefus ar y tŷ.
>> Mae'r tŷ yn chwerthin.
>> Mae'r tŷ yn gwenu.

> High-ability band.
>> Mae'r tŷ yn gwenu.
>> Mae gan y tŷ gêg.
>> Mae tŷ yn cael gwefusau.

> Average-ability band.
>> Mae tŷ yn cael cêg.
>> Mae tŷ yn gwerthin.
>> Mae'r tŷ yn hapus.

> Low-ability band.
>> Mae tŷ gyda cêg.
>> Mae tŷ has got a mouth.
>> Smiling.

Picture 2 showed a member of Jacques Cousteau's underwater exploration team wearing an inflated rubber diving-suit. Here are some of the responses.

> Native speakers.
>> Mae'r dyn 'na'n dew.
>> Mae'n dew.
>> Mae'r boy yn dew.
>
> High-ability band.
>> Mae dyn hwn yn dew.
>> Mae y dyn yn tew.
>> Mae dyn yn cael siwt nofio fawr.
>
> Average-ability band.
>> Mae dyn yn fawr.
>> Mae bachgen yn fat.
>> Mae dyn yn gwisgo siwt mawr.
>
> Low-ability band.
>> Mae dyn yn fawr.
>> Mae dyn yn mawr, mawr, mawr.
>> Mae dyn yn dew.

Picture 3, picture of the week in an American newspaper, showed a youth sitting at the side of a busy road in Los Angeles with nothing on, his clothes folded beside him. Here are some of the responses.

> Native speakers.
>> Dyw'r dyn ddim yn gwisgo dim.
>> Mae'r dyn 'na'n borcyn.
>> Mae dyn yn eistedd ar y pafin a dim byd arno fe.
>
> High-ability band.
>> Mae dyn ar y stryd a does dim arno fe.
>> Does dim dillad gan y dyn.
>> Mae'r dyn ddim gyda dillad.
>
> Average-ability band.
>> Y dyn ddim yn cael dillad arno.
>> Mae dyn yn . . . gyda dim . . . gyda gwisgo dim.
>> Mae e dim cael clothes on.
>
> Low-ability band.
>> Mae bachgen yn y stryd gyda no clothes.
>> Mae dyn a nothing ar.
>> He's naked.

These examples illustrate the different levels of response among the learners and how they differ from the native speakers. The main hindrance to expression among the learners was restricted vocabulary, even at this simple level. Pictures 1 and 3 also illustrate the great difficulty experienced by learners in mastering the Welsh idiom denoting possession. The use of 'gyda' in the wrong position, or alternatively the use of 'yn cael', occurs frequently in several test units. The high frequency of occurrence of this idiom should give it a high priority in the teaching programme. This pattern should be introduced early and its use should be practised regularly.

Unit 6

The pictorial material for this unit was taken from *Scope Picture Book Stage 1*.[8] Pupils were required to describe the differences between two pictures. These differences related to the number, colour and position of objects and people and entailed the expression of such ideas as different, the other side, right and left, behind, in front of and open and closed. It was not an easy exercise even for the native speakers. The pictures themselves are difficult to reproduce but the following sample transcripts will convey some idea of what was required and of what kinds of response were obtained.

A native speaker—Mae'r fenyw yr ochr 'na, a lawr man hyn mae hi'r ochr 'na. Mae hon 'na'n gwisgo teeshirt coch, a'r un 'na'n glas. Un cwpan sy man'na a dau man'na. Y teledu'n wahaniaeth—dyn a menyw man'na menyw man'na. Teeshirt coch 'da hwn, a un glas 'da fe, man'na. Pedair orange man'na a pum orange a banana man'na. Y calendar ar y dau a'r calendar ar y pump. Mae'r llyfr 'na'n frown a'r llyfr 'na'n felyn. Rhain 'na'n goch a'r rhain'na'n wyrdd. Mae curtain yn ga' man'na ac yn agor man'na. O ie, mae weiar yn mynd draw tu nôl man'na, ac mae'n mynd o flaen hwn man'na. Mae hwn'na'n orange a mae hwn'na'n las.

A high ability Project pupil—Ar y teledu mae llun ddim yn . . . mae llun A yn lliw a mae llun B ddim yn lliw. A ar y calendar mae llun A yn dau o July a ar llun B mae calendar yn pump o Gorffenn . . . Ar llun B mae dwy cwp a soser ar y bwrdd a ar llun A mae ddim, mae un cwp a soser. Yn y llyfrgell yn llun A mae dwy llyfr glas a un llyfr goch a yn llun B mae dwy llyfr glas a un llyfr melyn. A mae, yn llun B mae pump llyfr gwyrdd a yn llun A mae pump llyfr goch. A ar y teledu ar llun A mae button cyntaf . . . what's straight up? . . . a second across a'r trydydd up. Yn y llun A mae geneth yn cael gwallt gwyn a jumper goch a ar llun B mae geneth yn cael gwallt du a frock glas a belt, a ar llun A mae geneth yn y . . . maen nhw'n cael jumper glas a yn llun B maen nhw'n cael jumper goch. Ar llun A mae lampshade yn oren a ar B mae lampshade yn glas. Ar llun A mae taid yn eistedd ar y chwith a ar llun B taid yn eistedd ar y dde. Ar A mae . . . be' dy cushion? ar y dde a ar llun B mae ar y chwith. A llun A mae curtains wedi'u cau a ar llun B mae curtains yn agor.

An average Project pupil—Mae un cwp ar y bwrdd a mae dau ar y bwrdd. Mae'r lamp yn oren a mae lamp yn glas. Mae pillow ar y right a mae pillow ar y left. Mae calendar yn dweud July dau a mae calendar yn dweud July pump. Mae weiar yn mynd 'nol i teledu a mae weiar yn mynd i front i teledu. Mae llyfr yn gwyrdd a mae llyfr yn coch. Mae llyfr yn brown a mae llyfr yn melyn. Mae hair yn gwyn a mae hair yn brown. Mae curtains yn open. Mae knob yn pwyntio lawr a mae knob yn pwyntio i fyny.

A low-ability Project pupil—Mae yn different a mae picture ar y television yn different. Mae dyn ar y picture yn A, a B does dim dyn. Mae cwp yn A a dau cwp in B . . . I got that wrong . . . In A mae un cwp, in B mae dau cwp. A mae lampshade yn different. Mae lyfr yn y picture A yn coch, a in B mae . . . banana yn B a no banana yn A. Yn y picture A mae dau July a in B mae pump July. A mae cushion yn left yn B a on A on the right. Mae lampshade yn B yn coch a in A . . . A yn y T.V. mae yn different. Mae yn B ac yn A mae'n different. Mae'r wire over y bwrdd yn A ac yn B mae'r wire ar y llawr. A on A mae belt ar y geneth a ar B there's no belt ar geneth.

Even among native speakers response was often demonstrative, the pupil pointing to the difference rather than putting it precisely into words. The nature of response was similar among Project pupils, but the less able were often handicapped by lack of vocabulary. Whereas colour and number caused little difficulty, ideas like 'open' and 'closed', 'up' and 'across', 'behind' and 'in front of' proved more difficult. The responses quoted above also illustrate the common errors of grammar and syntax, e.g. 'Mae dwy llyfr glas' and 'Mae geneth yn cael gwallt du'. The last transcript is typical of the low-ability group in the large amount of English used and also in the ease with which these pupils switched from one language to another within sentences.

Unit 7

The last unit required pupils to re-tell a story which they had just heard on tape, while looking at a page of pictures which illustrated the story (v. Appendix B(5)). These pictures were also taken from *Scope Picture Book Stage 1.* This unit was administered to the group of native speakers as well as to the Project pupils. The following transcripts are reproduced to give the reader an idea of the different levels of response obtained from each group. This time the responses of two native speakers are quoted. The first native speaker is a pupil in a traditional Welsh school in rural Wales. The second native speaker is a pupil in a Welsh school in an anglicized town in Glamorgan. Before reading the following five versions, the reader is advised to read the transcript of the story which the children listened to, and which is reproduced in Appendix B(5).

Native speaker 1—Pan oedd John yn postio llythyr yn y Swyddfa Post, daeth dau ddyn mewn trwy'r drws a sannau am eu pennau. Sylwodd y ddau ddyn bod John ddim tu ol y drws ac oedd dau bag arian yn eu llaw nhw. Y dyn oedd . . . gododd ei ddwylo i fyny. A pan oedd y dau ddyn yn mynd allan, roedd John yn ffonio'r swyddfa heddlu. Ac fe ddaeth yr heddlu ac oedd y car yn mynd yn gyflym. Pan ddaeth y ddau ddyn fe welodd car yr heddlu groes y ffordd ac fe droiodd i stryd arall. Cyn bo hir fe gwrddon â gwartheg. Ac roedd rhaid iddyn nhw stopio. Cyn bo hir fe ddalodd yr heddlu lan ac fe aeth a nhw . . . i rywle . . . ac fe siglodd yr heddlu llaw gan . . . gyda John gan gweud 'Diolch yn fawr'.

Native speaker 2—Mae John yn postio llythyr mewn banc pan ddaeth dau leidr i mewn â dau hosan neilon am eu pennau. Daeth dau lleidr i mewn a heb sylwi John, yr oeddent wedi mynd at y cownter ac yr oeddent wedi gael drylliau nhw allan. Yr oedd y dyn tu ôl i'r cownter wedi rhoi ei ddwylo i fyny ac yr oeddent wedi . . . y lladron wedi mynd â bagiau o arian, a tra roeddent yn mynd i'r car yr oedd John yn ffonio'r heddlu. Ac tra oe'n nhw'n mynd, fe welon car yr heddlu'n dod tu ôl iddynt. A pan yr oeddent yn mynd, oe'n nhw wedi gweld plismon a'i law i fyny. Fe aeth y lladron mewn i stryd arall. Yr oeddent wedi mynd mewn i stryd arall ac yr oeddent yn mynd i'r wlad. Ar y ffordd yr oeddent wedi gweld gwartheg yng nghanol yr heol. Roedd rhaid iddynt stopio'r car. Tra roeddent wedi stopio, yr oedd plismon wedi dod ac yr oeddent wedi dal y lladron. Yr oedd lladron wedi mynd i'r

117

jail ac yr oedd un plismon wedi mynd a siglo llaw â John a diolch . . . a rhoi diolch iddo am helpu i ddal y lladron.

A high-ability Project pupil—Roedd John yn postio llythyr yn Swyddfa Post. Pan oedd o'n postio llythyr daeth dwy dyn i fewn gyda . . . ar eu . . . Roedd ddim yn gweld John a roedd tu ôl i'r drws. Roedd guns yn eu dwylo. Cododd dyn Swyddfa Post, cododd ei dwylo, a . . . what's they took the money? Rhedodd y dynion tu allan i fewn i'r car. Ac rhedodd John i'r telephone box a ffoniodd police. Pan oedd y police wedi cyrraedd, roedd y dynion just yn mynd. The police put a car. Roedd y car gyda'r dynion i fewn yn troi i lawr ffordd arall. Roedden nhw wedi mynd i'r wlad, ond ar y ffordd roedd buwch yn . . . ar y ffordd yn blocio y, y, ffordd y dynion. Pan oedd y, y buwch yn mynd o gwmpas y car modur, cyrrodd y police ac roedd wedi dal y dynion. Roedd y policeman yn shakio dwylo gyda John ac yn dweud diolch iddo fo am ei help.

An average Project pupil—Mae John yn mynd i Swyddfa'r Post a mae John yn rhoi ei letter yn y bocs a mae dau ddyn yn mynd, yn dod yn y Swyddfa Post a mae ddyn mynd i cownter a mae yn dweud i ddyn rhoi ei dwylo i fyny. Mae dyn yn rhoi yr arian i ddyn a mae yn mynd i car. Mae ddyn dim yn gweld John yn mynd i allan a mae John yn ffonio y police a mae police yn dod, yn mynd ar ol y dyn a mae police yn rhoi car ar yr heol a mae ddyn police yn rhoi ei dwylo i fyny. A mae car yn mynd i street arall a mae car yn mynd . . . beth yw down? yr heol, a mae buwch yn, ar yr heol, a mae ddyn yn y, mynd yn y . . . beth yw middle? o buwch. A mae ddyn police yn mynd i ddyn i . . . beth yw jail? A mae ddyn police yn dweud diolch yn fawr i John.

A low-ability Project pupil—Postio llyth. Bocs post. A mae dyn yn robbio post office a mae John yn ffonio i police a mae car yn mynd o dan y street a car yn turnio i corner a mynd y stryd. A mae buwch yn stopio i car a mae police yn thankio John.

The last version of the story quoted above illustrates one way in which the below-average pupil avoided some of the difficulties of relating the story. This pupil compressed the story into a short space, including only the barest essentials, and assimilated English words into his narrative with a confidence one could not but admire. The young learner must, after all, wonder why 'ffonio' and 'stopio' are acceptable, while 'turnio' and 'thankio' are not. Others in this band related the story more fully, but in order to do this switched frequently from Welsh to English. The number of English words used on average by pupils in the lowest band was forty-eight. The upper and middle bands used on average nine and ten English words respectively.

Although the pupils were asked simply to re-tell the story and were not asked to attempt to reproduce the words they had heard, it was interesting to analyse how many features of the tape-recorded story did actually appear in the children's versions of the story. This analysis was carried out within four groups, i.e. the native speakers and the three bands of Project pupils. Thirty-seven features of the original story, excluding all the nouns, were listed and note was made of whether each one occurred at least once in each child's version of the story. The results can be seen in the table in Appendix C. The average number of features used by each group, 14, 9.16, 4.91 and 1.50 respectively, points to the difference between them. But more interesting is a comparison of which features are used or not used by each group.

In the group of native speakers, instances were found of all the verb tenses listed, all types of subordinate clause, all adverbs and adverbial phrases except 'tua'r wlad' and all prepositions and prepositional phrases except 'wrth' and 'o'u blaen nhw'. However an inspection of the transcripts of native speakers 1 and 2 quoted above will reveal a distinct difference in their use of past tenses in the narrative. Native speaker 1 consistently uses the perfect tense for his narration, while native speaker 2 makes much more use of periphrastic forms.

In the above-average group of Project pupils, the most frequently-used verb form was 'mae . . . yn', followed by 'mae . . . wedi' and 'roedd . . . yn'. Only four instances of the perfect occurred, three of those occurring in one transcript. There were five instances of use of a subordinate clause. Most of the adverbs and prepositions were used, but 'tua'r wlad' and 'o'u blaen nhw' were again absent. Indeed these phrases did not appear in any of the groups.

The average group told their stories almost exclusively in the present tense and the recurring sentence pattern was 'mae . . . yn '. Only one instance of a subordinate clause was found. There was less variety of adverb and preposition than in the previous two groups. The only prepositions extensively used were the commonest ones 'yn' and 'i'.

The below-average group shows a very restricted use of language. The only verb form used was 'mae . . . yn'. There were no subordinate clauses used. None of the adverbs or adverbial phases appeared, and only three prepositions 'yn', 'i' and 'wrth'. It has already been noted that extensive use of English was made in this group.

A great deal of analysis of the transcribed material could be carried out, but it is felt that the responses reproduced in this section serve well enough the purpose of describing, in sample form at least, the levels of attainment of these pupils in the second language. The materials and situations chosen to try out the oral powers of these pupils were an arbitrary selection, but they served as some kind of yardstick against which to measure their powers of expression. They do not pretend to be an exhaustive or a scientific test, but the bands of pupils who took part in the exercise are fairly sharply differentiated in their performance. The reader can make his own judgement about the levels of competence attained by these pupils by the age of nine. It is regrettable that the span of the Project's operation did not extend far enough to allow such measurements to be made in the top classes of the junior schools. Only then could one confidently report on how far along the road to bilingualism such children can be taken before they leave their primary schools.

PROFILES OF HIGH ACHIEVEMENT

It is felt that the most fitting conclusion to a report of this kind would be an attempt to portray the way in which the Bilingual Education Project has operated in one or two real-life situations which the practising teacher can compare with and relate to his own teaching situation. Two schools have been selected where it is felt the Project has been satisfactorily implemented at both infant and junior levels. To preserve their anonymity they will be referred to as schools A and B. They are contrasted in some aspects of their background, although they also share common features. It is hoped that the following two profiles will illuminate some of the remarks and observations made in the preceding sections of this report.

School A

The infant school. School A consists of infant and junior schools under separate head teachers but until recently they were both housed in the same school building and shared the same hall. The building is an old-fashioned one, but its potential was fully exploited. Full use was made by the infant school of corridor and

120

even cloakroom area, and activity flowed from classrooms to corridor. Wall space was fully used and any visitor to the infant school was immediately struck by the enormous murals, consisting of gay and charming collage work on the theme of some story or current area of interest. These linked the children's craft activities to their other interests and when completed contributed greatly to the gaiety of the school's atmosphere.

The school, like so many of the Project schools, is situated in a small seaside town with only one primary school, so the pupils have a fairly mixed socio-economic background. The town is undergoing a fairly rapid process of anglicisation which is reflected in the school population. There is still a fairly high level of Welshness in the community surrounding the school and the linguistic background cannot be said to be typical of most of the schools which have participated in the Project. However the Project is likely to be adopted in many schools whose situation is similar to that of school A. This school contains a Welsh stream to cater for the education of pupils whose parents wish them to be educated primarily through the medium of Welsh, but the numbers in this stream are rapidly shrinking. Few of the pupils entering school now have two Welsh-speaking parents, and even some of those who do are not being placed in the Welsh stream. The school contains a small proportion of pupils who belong to the first generation of their families not to be brought up naturally Welsh-speaking. It was to meet this situation, in fact, that the Bilingual Education Project was first adopted in this school. In the junior school class about whom background information was collected in the session 1973-74, four out of twenty-two pupils had two Welsh-speaking parents and a further six had one Welsh-speaking parent.

When the Project was first adopted in this school both the head teacher and her staff were favourably disposed towards the programme and their efforts and enthusiasm have undoubtedly contributed greatly to the successful implementation of the Project. By now the Project has been implemented for about seven years in the infant school and during that period has undergone disturbances of the kind that can happen in any school. First, apart from the head teacher herself, the entire infant school staff changed at the same time at the end of one school year. Not long afterwards the infant school removed to a new building, an event which had long been looked forward to, but which nevertheless brought a certain amount of disturbance in its train. The head teacher herself has provided continuity in this situation, has carefully introduced new members of staff to the application of the bilingual programme and remains as convinced as ever of the usefulness and potential of such an educational programme.

The Project is introduced in the reception class of the school, but not until the second half-term of the year. The school feels that a settling-in period of a few weeks is desirable before the children are introduced to a second language. This is done through the play activities common in reception classes and in the course of the year Welsh is used to accompany a wide variety of these, including dance, mime, movement, mathematical experience of shape and size, craft work and even stories where the narrative is amply illustrated by visual materials. Organised group activity is not carried on with the younger children in this school, but is largely postponed until they reach the top infant class.

The school reports that understanding of the second language grows very rapidly and the reception class teacher is very soon able to give instructions in Welsh and expect response to them. Most of the response in the youngest class, however, is in deed rather than in word. Response in Welsh is very sparse at this level. When it occurs, it consists mainly of one word or short phrase responses, with the occasional use of sentences. The children cannot yet ask the teacher questions in Welsh. Pupils who had followed the Project for about four months were observed listening to the teacher talking about a book with large, coloured figures of a boy and girl, and then confidently giving brief answers to questions such as 'Beth ydy hwn?' 'Pa liw ydy hwn?' 'Beth mae'r ferch yn ei wneud?' 'Ble mae'r bachgen yn sefyll?'

During their second year the same kind of activities are continued and amplified. Comparison of size and shape is introduced. Craft work can be a little more ambitious as the children mature. Class organisation continues on the same lines, the whole class being used most often as a unit for second-language work. Pupils who had followed the Project for a year and four months were observed being questioned about a snowman book. They could answer questions like 'Beth sy gyda'r dyn eira?' 'Oes pib gyda'r dyn eira?' 'Oes menyg gyda chi?' 'Ydy Dadi'n smocio pib?' 'Ydych chi'n hoffi gwneud dyn eira?' The past tense is beginning to be used at this stage, but the children are still much more at home with the present tense. Verbal response increases during this year and to help the children gain confidence in expressing themselves in Welsh the teacher sometimes asks them to re-tell a story, each child contributing a little to the narrative.

During their third year pupils gain greatly in confidence in using Welsh and by now many will spontaneously ask the teacher questions in Welsh as well as replying in Welsh when spoken to. As reading and writing skills are established, the pupils often show a desire to read and write in Welsh as well as in English. However they still do not naturally communicate with each other in Welsh, nor do they speak to the children in the Welsh stream in Welsh. Group activity is organised in this year-group, so that in the second-language session pupils take part in a succession of activities after the class activity with the teacher. These group activities are very thoroughly prepared and the pupils are well trained to participate in them even when the teacher is not there to direct them. Some of the group activities relate to the current theme of study. When this year-group was observed the current theme was the story of Goldilocks. This theme was continued through several activities other than simply listening to the story being told. It formed the basis of craft sessions during which a large colourful mural was produced illustrating the characters and setting of the story. It was also used as the basis for dramatic activity and the pupils could act the story using simple costumes and props. A narrator outlined the story, and the characters supplied mime and dialogue. Of the seven group activities observed in this class, three were based on the Goldilocks story, the acting activity mentioned above, a group of children talking about the mural, each one taking a turn in asking questions of the others, and a board game created by the teacher and based on the story. This game practised reading skill, as the pupils took cards from a pile, read out the instructions and then carried them out. They were obviously well trained in the rules and conduct of the game and played with discipline and concentration. Other board games which had been introduced earlier with other activities occupied other groups and in all cases the children were well trained in the rules and rituals of the game and had thoroughly mastered the language which accompanied these activities. However it was noticed that if they wished to depart from the formulae of the game, they switched to English. If a comment was made, or an explanation given, it was in English. 'He doesn't want five though, he wants four' someone was heard to explain to a child who had not realised why the player had not moved his counter. The fact that this remark was made in English was probably not due to an inability to say it in Welsh. In fact another group game played in this class, a Lotto game, required each pupil to describe the picture on the card offered and then say either 'Rydw i eisiau . . .' or 'Dydw i ddim eisiau . . .' Perhaps the formality of the board game does not lend itself to extending language, but such activity is a useful and enjoyable way of reinforcing language patterns. Another dramatic activity used with small groups is the acting out of situations like having a tea-party. Here again the children practise the ritual language of such a situation and the rehearsal of these questions and answers as they take turns in playing the different roles gives remarkable fluency and expertise in handling these expressions.

The school takes advantage of the presence of the Welsh-stream and its teacher by 'lending' the Welsh-medium teacher to the older infant pupils for occasional story sessions. One such session was observed in which the children were told a Bible story, illustrated by a wall-picture and a set of coloured pictures made by the teacher, each one sub-titled by a section of a simple story script. Comprehension was tested by questioning and the pupils answered readily in Welsh. Reading skill was exercised as sometimes the group and sometimes an individual would read a sub-title aloud.

The presence of the Welsh stream, admittedly very small in numbers, does not appear to exert any influence on the social use of Welsh in the school. A great deal of incidental use of Welsh is made by the staff in the corporate life of the school and occasionally during the school day. But outside lesson time when the pupils are removed from the teachers' influence, English remains the language of social intercourse. Nevertheless by the time they leave their infant school, these pupils have a very high level of comprehension of Welsh and considerable mastery of the basic patterns recommended for use in the infant schools in the Project literature. Moreover their general attitude towards their activities through the medium of their second language is one of confidence and enjoyment.

The junior school. When these pupils reach the junior school they are fortunate in having a head teacher and teachers who are as convinced of the feasibility of a bilingual programme of education as were the staff of the infant school. The organisation of the junior school is slightly different from that of the infant school. There is again a small Welsh-medium stream, then a much larger stream, the main body of the school, in which the Bilingual Education Project is implemented. But there is also a remedial class for slow learners in which the Project is not implemented.

The head teacher involves himself in the implementation of the Project in each year-group, and himself takes an active part in the preparation of materials in the second language. He has prepared a series of duplicated workbooks on a variety of subjects, mostly geographical, historical or sociological. These are used with the older children to consolidate their lessons and discussions on each topic. Using the workbooks themselves is a formal, intellectual exercise and demands a fairly high level of literacy in the second language. In the group test of Welsh language skills administered in 1974 to the second-year junior classes, this school's average was much higher than the mean for the whole group of Project schools taking the test, and among the highest even among those in which the Project was judged to be implemented satisfactorily.

However, not all the work done through the medium of the second language is of a formal nature. One highly successful project on a theme of local interest involved the whole school in visits to the local harbour. Pupils were prepared for these visits in class. They discussed their fathers' occupations, the traffic that used the harbour, different modes of transport, the history of shipping, did simple scientific experiments with water after discussing the Plimsoll line, made graphs based on traffic counts, and used music and drama to re-enact episodes from local history.

These pupils use their second language in such a variety of study contexts that their level of comprehension rises rapidly. Their oral expression, too, is above average. The school's records show an ambitious programme for extending language mastery by introducing in the first year, for example, common subordinate clauses such as 'achos bod hi' and 'sy'n agos', and forms like 'ganddyn nhw' and 'yn eu herbyn'. In the second year verb forms such as 'fe fydda i', 'fe fyddwn ni' and 'cael ei ddefnyddio' are introduced. In the third year forms like 'fe fyddech chi', 'pe bai', 'yn arfer bod', 'fel eu bod nhw' and 'rhaid' are recorded. As well as these, record has been kept of the introduction of such vital features as 'rhy', 'un ar ben y llall', 'gormod', 'rhan fwya', 'bron i gyd', 'ar ei ben ei hun' and 'gyda'i gilydd'. It is difficult to know, of course, how much of this language has been fully assimilated into the pupils' own speech. This school did not appear in the samples used for oral testing either at infant or at junior level. However, tape-recorded examples of pupils' speech are available and give the impression of a high level of fluency among the better pupils. Some of the material reveals an impressive use of quite specialised vocabulary, but what is more impressive is the easy handling of comparison—'Mae John yn byw'n agosach i'r ysgol na Richard' and 'Maen nhw'n dalach na chi', and the perfect construction of a complex sentence such as the following, 'Nage, baner sy'n dweud bod y llong yn barod i fynd allan yw hon'.

Both infant and junior schools feel that the Project programme is one that can be highly successful if implemented under the right conditions. They are in a position to provide these conditions, and feel that such a bilingual programme meets the needs of a generation of children who would perhaps without it be growing up with little or no knowledge of a language which was, until fairly recently, the first language of the community in which they live.

School B
The infant school. The background of this school is very different from that of school A. It is a larger school, having a two-class entry, and is situated in an industrialised town with rural surroundings. Most of the pupils are drawn from the lower categories of socio-economic background. The town is very anglicised, but does contain a minority of Welsh-speakers. The presence of this minority, however, has little effect on the population of this school, as there is a Welsh-medium school which caters for the needs of pupils of Welsh-speaking parents. Very few of these choose to send their children to school B. In the junior class about which background information was sought in 1974, only one pupil out of twenty-nine had two Welsh-speaking parents. A further four had one Welsh-speaking parent.

Like school A, infant and junior schools are separate schools under different head teachers, but the two schools are on adjoining campuses. Another point of similarity is that the infant head teacher adopted the Bilingual Education Project in her school with enthusiasm and determination, indeed at a time when she herself was the only bilingual member of her staff. The organisation of the Project in the school has evolved with the changing circumstances. At first the head teacher herself was responsible for all the second-language sessions, which she conducted in her room. As more bilingual teachers have been appointed to the staff, the Project programme has taken its place in the class work of one class of pupils in each year-group, beginning in the reception class. When the Project was adopted, each year-group was divided into two classes on the basis of age, and the Project programme was implemented in the younger class in each year-group. More recently, vertical grouping has been introduced in the first two years, so that there have been two groups with an age-range of four to six years and a top class of six- to seven-year-olds following the Project programme.

In the reception class Welsh is introduced through such activities as water and sand play, blocks, farm and zoo activities, as well as seasonal topics which arise in the course of the year. Colour, shape and number are experienced and the language to accompany them is assimilated through these activities. The basic present tense sentence pattern 'Mae'r . . .' is introduced, and the question forms 'Ble mae . . .?' 'Beth mae . . . yn ei wneud?' 'Ydy'r . . .?' and 'Pa liw ydy . . .?' The commonest prepositions, 'yn', 'ar' and 'o dan', are introduced. Regular classroom greetings and instructions are taught in the second language. The listening books devised by the Project are used, particularly those relating to seasonal topics.

In the second year, sentence patterns are extended to include 'Oes', 'Nac oes, does dim . . .', 'Rydw i . . .', 'Rydych chi . . .', 'Mae gen i . . .', 'Rydw i eisiau . . .', 'Dydw i ddim eisiau . . .' Questions using 'faint' and 'sawl' are introduced. Activities are extended as the children mature. Experience of size and shape includes ideas like long and short, fat and thin. The senses of sight and hearing form the basis of interesting work and the children learn to discuss what they see and hear both in school and in other settings outside school, e.g. the garden, the farm and the seaside. Feeling objects and materials also extends their descriptive vocabulary. Use is made of tape-recorded sound-effects in this area of the work. Considerable use of the listening books, of other stories and songs and of craft activities linked to current interests ensures that the pupils' experience of the second language is gained in a wide variety of context. The children are also trained to play games in Welsh some for use in the classroom and some to be played in the playground.

In the third year the past tenses of verbs are introduced, 'Mae . . . wedi', 'Roedd . . .' and 'Fe fues i . . .' Patterns previously introduced like 'Mae gen i . . .' are reviewed. There is further use of the listening books, more ambitious craft activity, a widening of the children's repertoire of songs and games, mathematical work on sets and graph-making and topical projects linked to seasonal events. By the end of this year, the commonest prepositions have all been presented, i.e. 'yn', 'ar', 'o dan', 'wrth', 'tu ôl', 'o flaen', 'o gwmpas' and 'dros'.

The top infant class tested for listening comprehension in 1973 showed a high level of understanding and their class average was higher than the mean for all Project schools. This class did not appear in the sample which took the oral test. By the time they are seven, the children are prepared to answer the teacher and visitors to the class in Welsh. However, spontaneous conversation among the pupils themselves is carried on solely in English.

The junior school. Before the first cohort of Project pupils passed into their junior school, the headmaster of that school had visited the infant school and had discussions with the headmistress in readiness for setting up the continuation of the bilingual programme in his school. Only half the intake would have followed the Project programme and the junior school had a more than adequate supply of bilingual staff to meet their needs. At the time of writing the Project has reached the fourth year in the junior school, so the younger junior classes by now have considerable experience in its implementation. The present head teacher feels the Project programme has made a good contribution to the children's education. He is pleased with their progress in the second language and ensures that Welsh as well as English has its place in the life of the school. He encourages extra-curricular activities through the medium of Welsh and has established a branch of Urdd Gobaith Cymru in the school. He was quite open-minded about trying out the Project programme in its early days and wished to compare attainment in Welsh among the Project pupils in his school with that of those who learned Welsh as a subject. He is more than satisfied that the Project's use of Welsh as a medium of instruction has produced a higher level of language mastery than any other method of language teaching of which he has experience. He also feels sure that the pupils' general development has not suffered in any way.

In the first-year class which has had two different teachers since 1971, the following themes have been chosen as a basis for second-language activities: the milkman, the policeman, the Wombles, a visit to a safari park, homes, water, collecting blackberries and making jam, traditional Welsh stories. It is gratifying to note that many of these areas of study gave rise to visits outside school—to a farm, a police station, a safari park and a walk in the country to pick blackberries. These all make a vivid and enjoyable basis for classroom discussion and activities. After the visit to a police station, for example, the pupils, who had observed the fingerprint unit during their visit, enjoyed taking each other's fingerprints, they made models of a police car and radio, modelled a giant policeman, made puppets and used them for dramatic activity on this theme. The Wombles, of course, lent themselves to dressing-up, acting and singing, as well as model-making and the compiling of books illustrated by the children's paintings. Womble songs in

Welsh were composed by the teacher and sung with great enjoyment. These activities culminated in the acting of a Womble episode in the school concert. The project on water gave rise to a number of mathematical and scientific activities such as measurement of rainfall, experiments with water and the study of river life. In all these activities opportunities are taken to establish control of the past tenses of verbs, both imperfect and perfect. This can be introduced quite naturally when discussing visits. More adjectives and prepositions are introduced. The days of the week and language of the weather are used in date and weather charts filled in daily.

The second-year class continues this pattern of basing many of the second-language activities on visits. This year-group had visited a fire-station, the post office and the town park and has gone shopping, in studying such topics as the fire-engine, our town, the post, food and autumn. Practical activities in school also play their part. This class made bread as their contribution to the school's thanksgiving service in the autumn, and photographs were taken of the different stages of this activity. The pupils talked and wrote about it afterwards. The visit to the post office provides a good example of the variety of activities which can arise from one theme. The pupils learned to address an envelope, made a classroom post-box and delivered letters, studied what happens to a letter on its journey from sender to recipient, using the poster produced by the Post Office, studied the history of the postal service and dramatised a highwayman's holdup. In the course of these activities all the language patterns previously learnt were reviewed. Special attention was given to the past tenses of verbs, new adjectives were introduced e.g. 'glân', 'budr', 'drwg', 'da' and 'blasus' and more plural forms of nouns were taught.

The teacher in charge of the third year was a newcomer to the work of the Project when the writer visited the school in 1974, the session in which the Project reached third-year junior level. He confessed to having been completely baffled at the beginning of the year, not knowing what kind of task was facing him. He felt that he was not adequately prepared for the work, but received a lot of advice and help from the teachers of the classes below his. His previous experience of children learning Welsh as a second language led him to expect too little of his pupils. He soon came to realise that they had attained a standard of comprehension and speech far higher than he had expected and he had to adjust himself to their standard of attainment. This class did work relating to seasonal events like the harvest and Christmas, made a map of their town and studied some local history and legends, followed up in class discussions a visit by some of the pupils to a Welsh camp, studied the time and clocks, and worked on the theme of helping in the garden. Apart from the varied vocabulary that arose from these themes, expressions relating to time were taught, dates and days of the week reviewed, and the past tenses of verbs again needed much practice.

When the second-year junior pupils were tested in Welsh in 1974, the pupils of this school achieved a class average higher than the Project mean score. More than a quarter of the class had exceptionally high scores in *Prawf Cymraeg*. None of these pupils had any Welsh in their immediate family background. These same pupils also had above-average scores in English (ranging from 104 to 127) and in English reading (ranging from 109 to 125). The class average scores in the battery of five NFER tests administered in 1974 were as follows:

Reading BD — 101
Mathematics B — 100
English Progress B2 — 101
Non-verbal BD — 105
Verbal BC — 102

All the teachers implementing the Project programme in this school were asked if they sensed any diminution of interest among their pupils when the medium of teaching and discussion was Welsh. None said they had felt this. One teacher said that newcomers to the school, who had no knowledge of Welsh, presented a problem, but all thought that the pupils who had followed a bilingual programme were just as interested in the work presented through the medium of the second language as in work they did in their mother-tongue.

Postscript

Schools A and B both adopted the Bilingual Education in its early days as a pilot study. This is one reason why they were selected for these profiles. In these schools the Project has had time to stabilise. Early difficulties have been solved, for the most part, but, on the other hand the aura of novelty, the added zest gained from doing something new, has had time to wear off. There were other reasons for their selection too. First, they both serve a cross-section of the population of their respective neighbourhoods and can be regarded as fairly representative of the national school population. Secondly, in cases A and B, the basic requirements for implementing the Project are present at both infant and junior levels. These schools illustrate how the Project has worked in two types of linguistic situation, one where the area is almost completely anglicised, and one where there is a residuum of Welsh. They have not been described with the purpose of setting them up as models, but rather to give the reader with no experience of the Project in action some insight into how it operates.

SUMMARY OF FINDINGS

1. A basic essential for the successful implementation of a programme of bilingual education is an adequate supply of bilingual teachers who are willing to participate in such a programme.

2. In the infant schools the allocation of adequate time to second language activities (ideally half the school day) proved to be a most important factor in second language attainment. Drastic curtailment of time devoted to work in the second language resulted in a low level of achievement in the second language.

3. On the whole infant schools or departments were readier to devote adequate time to second language activities than were junior schools or departments.

4. In junior schools where bilingual teachers had favourable attitudes towards using the second language as a medium of instruction in a variety of learning contexts, attainment in the second language was significantly higher than when the implementation of the Project programme was hampered by inflexibility, inadequate provision of time, unfavourable teacher attitudes or shortage of bilingual staff.

5. The skill of understanding speech in the second language was generally well established by the age of seven.

6. On the basis of a short oral test it was felt that speaking skills were fairly well established among the average and above-average pupils by the age of seven. Some pupils had poor speech skills by seven, however, and the range of attainment in speech was wider than the range of attainment in listening comprehension.

7. Emphasis on oral work in the junior schools and the lack of a firm policy regarding reading and writing in the second language made it difficult to assess adequately attainment in the area of reading and writing among the nine-year-olds. A rather difficult

131

test showed up a very wide range of ability, but with most of the pupils gaining rather low scores.

8. There is evidence of a consolidation and improvement of second language speech skills between the ages of seven and nine. Average and above-average pupils showed a fair degree of fluency by the age of nine and were usually undismayed by any deficiencies in their second-language vocabulary. Below-average pupils, however, were disappointing and cannot be said to have reached a speech level anywhere near that of native speakers.

9. The level of Welshness present in the background of the pupil and his school would seem to have some effect on his attainment of speech skills, but not on his attainment in other more passive areas of linguistic competence, except where the Project could not be implemented satisfactorily.

10. When top infant classes were tested in second-language listening comprehension and oral skills, there was no significant difference between the scores of pupils who had followed the Project for two years and those of pupils who had followed the Project for three years.

11. No evidence was found to suggest that general intellectual development and attainment in the basic subjects suffered in any way as a result of the implementation of the bilingual education programme. When samples of Project pupils were compared with control groups at the ages of seven and nine, no significant differences between the groups were found at either age-level in English, English reading, mathematics or non-verbal ability. In the verbal ability test administered to the nine-year-old pupils, only one significant difference between means was found. In the highest socio-economic category the Project group mean was significantly higher (at the 5 per cent level of significance) than that of the control group. In other socio-economic categories, however, there was no significant difference.

FLOW DIAGRAM TO ILLUSTRATE RESEARCH PROCEDURES

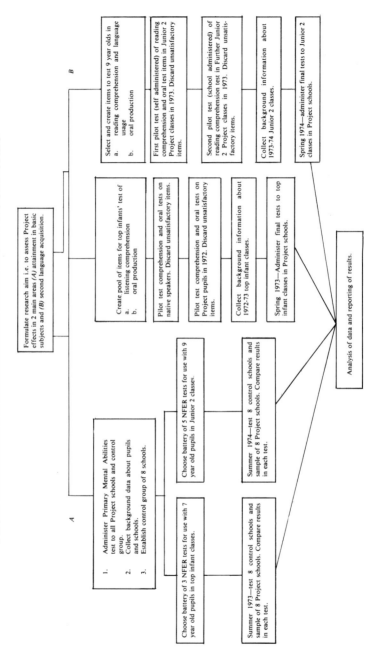

Formulate research aim i.e. to assess Project effects in 2 main areas *(A)* attainment in basic subjects and *(B)* second language acquisition.

A

1. Administer Primary Mental Abilities test to all Project schools and control group.
2. Collect background data about pupils and schools.
3. Establish control group of 8 schools.

Choose battery of 3 NFER tests for use with 7 year old pupils in top infant classes.

Choose battery of 5 NFER tests for use with 9 year old pupils in Junior 2 classes.

Summer 1973—test 8 control schools and sample of 8 Project schools. Compare results in each test.

Summer 1974—test 8 control schools and sample of 8 Project schools. Compare results in each test.

B

Select and create items to test 9 year olds in
a. reading comprehension and language usage
b. oral production

Create pool of items for top infants' test of
a. listening comprehension
b. oral production

First pilot test (self administered) of reading comprehension and oral test items in Junior 2 Project classes in 1973. Discard unsatisfactory items.

Pilot test comprehension and oral tests on native speakers. Discard unsatisfactory items.

Second pilot test (school administered) of reading comprehension test in Further Junior 2 Project classes in 1973. Discard unsatisfactory items.

Pilot test comprehension and oral tests on Project pupils in 1972. Discard unsatisfactory items.

Collect background information about 1973-74 Junior 2 classes.

Collect background information about 1972-73 top infant classes.

Spring 1974—administer final tests to Junior 2 classes in Project schools.

Spring 1973—Administer final tests to top infant classes in Project schools.

Analysis of data and reporting of results.

133

REFERENCES

1. Gittins Report, *Primary Education in Wales*, Central Advisory Council for Education (Wales), HMSO, 1967.

2. Schools Council, *Gweithgareddau i'r Plant Bach*, Schools Council Publications, 1975.

3. Thurstone, L. L. and T. G., *S.R.A. Primary Mental Abilities Test for Ages 5 to 7*, Science Research Associates Inc., 1953.

4. Chambers, E. G., *Statistical Calculation for Beginners*, Cambridge University Press, 1964, 34-45.

5. Kirk, S. A., McCarthy, J. J. and Kirk, W. D., *Illinois Test of Psycho-linguistic Abilities*, University of Illinois Press, 1968.

6. Schools Council, 'Dyn wrth ei Waith' (unpublished).

7. Sharp, D. *et al.*, *Attitudes to Welsh and English in the Schools of Wales* (Schools Council Research Studies), Macmillan/University of Wales Press, 1973.

8. Schools Council, *Scope, Stage 1: Picture Book*, Schools Council Publications, 1970.

ACKNOWLEDGEMENTS

Thanks are due to the following for the help they have given in many different ways: The Consultative Committee of the Bilingual Education Project; the Project Director, Mr G. E. Richards, and the field officers, Mrs W. Thomas, Miss G. Lloyd Evans, Miss G. Jones, Miss G. Parkinson, Mr J. Garnon and Mr A. Jones; the Chief Education Officers of all the counties in Wales; the head teachers, teachers and pupils of schools both within and outside the project; the Director, Mr E. Evans, and technical staff of the National Language Unit, Pontypridd; the secretarial staff of the Project; Mr Derrick Sharp, Director, Schools Council Project on Attitudes to Welsh and English in the schools of Wales; Mr E. T. Whittaker, Lecturer in Social Statistics, University College of Swansea; the staff of the Computation Centre, University College of Swansea; the artists, Mr J. Chamberlain, Mrs J. Chatfield and Mr M. Freeman.

Appendix A

The following N.F.E.R. tests were used to test Project and control groups of infant and junior pupils.

In top infant classes
> Picture Test A
> Reading Test BD
> English Progress Test A2

In second-year junior classes
> Reading Test BD
> English Progress Test B2
> Mathematics Test B
> Non-Verbal Ability Test BD
> Verbal Ability Test BC

The above tests are published by Ginn and Co. Ltd., for the National Foundation for Educational Research in England and Wales.

Appendix B.1

Items selected for final version * of *Prawf Gwrando a Deall,* a listening comprehension test for infants.

Item	Facility value	Discrimination value
Mae'r oen bach gwyn yn y cae.	70.41	0.55
Mae'r lori'n mynd i fyny'r rhiw.	67.01	0.32
Mae Dadi'n chwythu'r pwll padlo i fyny.	42.86	0.33
Mae'r plant yn gwneud castell tywod.	63.27	0.53
Mae'r ferch wedi gwisgo'i chot.	29.93	0.35
Mae'r bachgen yn y cwch.	73.13	0.53
Mae hi'n bwrw glaw.	62.24	0.47
Mae'r ferch yn mynd am dro yn y ferfa.	63.27	0.39
Dydy'r plant ddim yn chwarae yn iard yr ysgol.	37.76	0.37

*Two versions of this test were recorded, one for use in South Wales and one for use in North Wales. The above items appeared in the version used in South Wales.

Mae'r gweithwyr yn bwyta brechdanau.	51.36	0.39
Mae basged wag gyda'r plant.	52.04	0.30
Mae'r gŵyddau'n rhedeg ar ôl y ferch.	67.35	0.60
Dydy'r fuwch ddim yn y beudy.	62.59	0.57
Mae'r ferch o dan y goeden.	68.03	0.51
Does dim tywod yn y ferfa.	68.03	0.61
Mae'r plant wedi gwisgo i fyny.	33.33	0.33
Dydy'r ci ddim yn cnoi asgwrn.	50.68	0.52
Mae'r cregyn yn y bocs.	70.07	0.52
Mae Mami'n prynu cig.	47.96	0.47
Mae Mair wedi agor y drws.	58.84	0.43
Mae pedair ffenest yn y wal.	57.48	0.55
Mae'r bwced yn llawn.	46.94	0.49
Mae'r gath fach wedi torri'r plat.	56.80	0.41
Mae'r plant yn gallu gweld y môr.	50.34	0.54
Mae'r defaid yn y gorlan.	28.23	0.32
Dydy'r ci ddim yn cysgu.	71.43	0.74
Mae'r llawr yn wlyb.	53.74	0.44
Dydy'r plant ddim yn rhedeg.	61.22	0.68
Mae rhaw fawr gyda'r bachgen a rhaw fach gyda'r ferch.	57.82	0.72
Mae'r dyn yn arllwys tywod o'r ferfa.	47.62	0.35
Dydy'r ferch ddim yn magu dol.	52.38	0.68
Does dim simnai ar y to.	69.39	0.69
Mae'r plant yn cael wyau wedi'u berwi i frecwast.	58.84	0.47
Dydy'r morlo ddim yn nofio yn y llyn.	46.94	0.36
Mae moch yn y cae.	67.01	0.45
Dies dim llew yn y caets.	63.61	0.58
Mae llestri yn y cwpwrdd.	63.95	0.36
Mae Sian wedi rhoi'r doliau i gyd yn y gwely.	45.58	0.35
Dydy'r bachgen ddim yn gwisgo sgidiau glaw.	59.52	0.62
Mae'r eliffantod yn cerdded mewn cylch.	67.35	0.56
Dydy Mair ddim yn darllen llyfr.	64.97	0.59
Does dim seren ar y goeden Nadolig.	66.67	0.64

Dydy'r plant ddim wedi gwisgo i fyny.	53.06	0.39
Bachgan tal.	61.22	0.65
Ruban hir.	55.10	0.58
Coeden uchel.	44.90	0.44
Trowsus byr.	43.88	0.47
Cregyn pinc.	56.80	0.33
Blodau glas.	45.92	0.52
Tair cath fach.	37.76	0.30

B.1 (contd.) Sample page of pictures used in Prawf Gwrando a Deall.

Appendix B.2

Version of *Prawf Llafar* used in first stage of pilot test.

Picture 1: words used by tester   *Picture 2:* expected response

Un bloc.	Tri bloc.
Mae'r gath ar y gadair.	Mae'r gath o dan y gadair.
Un ci.	Dau gi.
Het Mami ydy hon.	Het Dadi ydy hon.
Mae Dadi'n fawr.	Mae'r babi'n fach.
Un llaw.	Dwy law.
Un plentyn.	Tri phlentyn.
Mae'r ferch yn cario'r bêl.	Mae'r bachgen yn cicio'r bêl.
Ffrog, ffrogiau; dyn; dafad.	Dynion; defaid.
Mae llew yn y caets.	Mae llewod yn y caets.
Rydyn ni'n bwyta bara.	Rydyn ni'n yfed llaeth.
Mae'r mwg yn mynd i fyny.	Mae'r glaw yn dod i lawr.
Rydyn ni'n chwarae yn ystod y dydd.	Rydyn ni'n cysgu yn (ystod) y nos.
Mae'r bachgen yn rhedeg.	Mae'r dyn yn cerdded.
Rydw i'n eistedd ar y gadair.	Rydw i'n gorwedd (cysgu) yn (ar) y gwely.
Mae'r bocs bach yn ysgafn.	Mae'r bocs mawr yn drwm.
Cot y babi ydy hon.	Cot y ferch ydy hon.
Rydyn ni'n gweld gyda'n llygaid.	Rydyn ni'n clywed gyda'n clustiau.
Mae'r gath yn rhedeg ar ôl y llygoden.	Mae'r gath wedi dal y llygoden.
Mae e'n mynd i roi'r darlun ar y wal.	Mae e wedi rhoi'r darlun ar y wal.
Mae llawer o flociau gyda'r bachgen.	Mae mwy o flociau gyda'r ferch.
Mae'r botel yma'n llawn.	Mae'r botel yma'n hanner llawn.
Mae'r bloc hwn yn fach; mae'r bloc hwn yn fwy;	. . . mwya(f)
dyma'r bloc . . .	
Mae'r bachgen yn mynd i fwyta'r bisgedi i gyd.	
Mae e eisiau un arall, ond . . .	. . . does dim (un) ar ôl.

Mae'r eliffant yn fwy na'r ceffyl . . .
Mae'r iâr yn . . .   llai na'r ceffyl.
Mae'r siocled yn felys. Mae'r   . . . sur.
lemwn yn . . .
Mae'r bachgen yn byw mewn   Mae'r aderyn yn byw mewn nyth.
tŷ.
Mae'r mochyn yn dew.   Mae'r pensil yn denau.
Dillad y ferch ydy'r rhain.   Dillad y bachgen ydy'r rhain.
Mae'r bachgen yn sefyll yn   Mae'r bachgen hwn yn eistedd
erbyn y wal.   ar y wal.
Mae'r aderyn yn hedfan yn yr   Mae'r pysgodyn yn nofio yn
awyr.   y dwr.
Mae un o'r plant wedi cwympo   . . . i gyd wedi cwympo lawr.
lawr. Maen nhw . . .
Mae'r bachgen yn mynd ar   Mae'r bechgyn yn mynd ar gefn
gefn mul.   mulod.
Mae hi'n rhoi ei bys yn y dwr.   Mae hi'n rhoi ei bysedd yn y dwr.
Mae hi'n mynd i gael torri'i   Mae hi wedi torri'i gwallt.
gwallt.

Appendix B.3

Facility values of test items in *Prawf Llafar* (final version).

Item	F.V.	Item	F.V.
Mae'r gath	0.91	-erch	0.55
o dan	0.39	ydy	0.52
y gadair	0.72	hon	0.33
Mae'r babi	0.69	Mae'r aderyn	0.53
'n	0.73	yn y nyth	0.33
f-	0.33	Word order	0.78
-ach	0.55	Dillad	0.69
Mae'r bachgen	0.80	y bachgen	0.69
yn cicio	0.51	ydy'r	0.49
'r bel	0.74	rhain	0.31
Ryd-	0.68	hwn	0.39
-yn ni'n	0.25	eistedd	0.65
yfed	0.21	ar y wal	0.74
llaeth	0.69	Mae'r pysgodyn	0.71
Ryd-	0.66	yn nofio	0.50
yn ni'n	0.19	yn	0.72
cysgu	0.69	y dŵr/môr/llyn	0.83

yn y nos	0.25	i gyd	0.09
cerdded	0.54	wedi	0.27
Mae e'n	0.47	m-	0.40
gorwedd	0.07	-awr	0.70
ar	0.58	d-	0.14
y gwely	0.62	-rwm	0.14
Cot y (word order)	0.87	llai	0.07
f-	0.07	na'r	0.12

The Schools Council has reproduced a limited number of copies of this test. Copies may be obtained on application to Dr. E. Price, Department of Education, University College of Swansea, Hendrefoilan, Swansea, SA2 7NB.

Appendix B.4

Prawf Cymraeg (a Welsh test for juniors).

Item facility values are inserted on the right hand side of the page.

Rhan 1

Read this passage carefully and answer the questions which follow it. Choose the correct answer (from A, B, C, or D), and put a ring around the letter in front of it.

Mae'n fore Sadwrn braf yn y gwanwyn, ac mae Geraint wedi codi'n gynnar. Mae e wedi ymolchi a gwisgo ac mae e'n paratoi i fynd i Lanfair. Mae'n llyncu'i frecwast ac i ffwrdd ag e.

Mae Ifan, ei ffrind, yn sefyll wrth yr arosfan. Mae'r ddau'n siarad am y gêm bêl-droed yn y dref. Tîm ysgol Cwmgwyn sy'n chwarae yn erbyn tîm eu hysgol nhw. Mae Ifan yn chwarae i dîm yr ysgol, ond mynd i wylio'r gêm mae Geraint.

O'r diwedd, mae'r bws yn dod, bum munud yn hwyr. Mae'r ffrindiau'n dringo i'r bws ac yn eistedd gyda'i gilydd yn agos i'r cefn.

Mae'r bws yn cyrraedd y dref am ugain munud i ddeg, ac mae Geraint yn mynd i gaffe wrth ochr gorsaf y bysiau cyn mynd i weld y gêm. Wrth gwrs, mae rhaid i Ifan fynd yn syth i'r ysgol i newid. Mae Geraint yn yfed cwpanaid o goffi, ac yn cyrraedd cae'r ysgol erbyn i'r gêm ddechrau am hanner awr wedi deg.

1. The phrase 'yn y gwanwyn' means—
    A. In the country
    B. in spring
    C. at the week-end
    D. in the holidays   0.35

2. How do you think Geraint ate his breakfast?
    A. He ate it slowly with enjoyment
    B. He gulped it down
    C. He left most of it
    D. He ate it on the way out   0.38

3. The phrase 'i ffwrdd ag e' means—
    A. to the road
    B. he is going away
    C. he runs out of the house
    D. off he goes   0.36

4. Geraint is going to the match—
    A. as a member of the Llanfair School team
    B. as a member of the Cwmgwyn School team
    C. as a reserve
    D. to watch the game   0.52

5. When the bus reaches the stop where Ifan and Geraint are
   waiting, it is—
    A. a few minutes early
    B. five minutes early
    C. five minutes late
    D. on time   0.22

6. The bus reaches Llanfair at—
    A. twenty minutes past ten
    B. ten o'clock
    C. half-past ten
    D. twenty minutes to ten   0.19

7. The two boys make their way to the school field—
    A. together, after having a cup of coffee
    B. separately, Geraint going first

C.   separately, Ifan going first
D.   together, immediately after reaching Llanfair   0.13

In this exercise you are asked to complete or to form sentences. The words needed are given below the line. Write out the words *in the correct order* above the line.

EXÁMPLE—

        Mae ysgol   yn y pentref

    A.   ysgol
    B.   mae

8.   yn y tŷ

    A.   'r bachgen
    B.   ddim
    C.   dydy   0.31

9.   Mae _____

    A.   y papur
    B.   darllen
    C.   yn gyflym
    D.   e'n   0.22

10.   Mae _____

    A.   da
    B.   Dafydd
    C.   fachgen
    D.   yn   0.29

11.   _____

    A.   bachgen
    B.   rhedeg
    C.   sy'n
    D.   sawl   0.34

12.   Fe _____

    A.   Mair
    B.   yn y dref
    C.   welais i   0.34

13. _____

_____ yn y prynhawn?

   A. gyda'r bechgyn
   B. chwarae
   C. 'r athro'n
   D. ydy
   E. pêl-droed   0.16

14. _____

   A. cot
   B. yn las
   C. mae
   D. ferch
   E. y   0.14

15. _____

   A. 'r piano
   B. dim
   C. canu
   D. sy'n
   E. Mr. Ifans   0.04

16. _____

   A. drwg
   B. ydy
   C. bachgen
   D. John   0.08

Choose the correct answer (from A, B, C or D) and put a ring around the letter in front of it. Like this—

EXAMPLE—

     Ydy'r bachgen yn rhedeg?
   A. Ydych
  Ⓑ Ydy
   C. Oes
   D. Ie

17. Gerddodd hi i'r ysgol ddoe?
    A. Oes
    B. Ie
    C. Ydw
    D. Do   0.34

18. Oeddech chi'n gwrando?
    A. Ydw
    B. Oeddech
    C. Oeddwn
    D. Oedd   0.22

19. Weloch chi John?
    A. Nage
    B. Nadda
    C. Nac ydw
    D. Nac ydych   0.29

20. Ydy'r plant yn yr ysgol?
    A. Ydy
    B. Oedden
    C. Ydyn
    D. Ydw   0.15

21. Oedd y plant yn hwyr yn dod i ginio?
    A. Oedden
    B. Ydyn
    C. Oeddwn
    D. Oedd   0.14

22. Bechgyn sy'n chwarae pêl-droed?
    A. Ydyn
    B. Ie
    C. Ydw
    D. Oeddwn   0.19

23. Dydych chi ddim wedi gweld Sioned?
    A. Nage
    B. Nac ydw
    C. Nac ydych
    D. Ie   0.39

24. Oes arian gyda chi?
    A. Ydw
    B. Oedd
    C. Oes
    D. Ydych   0.72

25. Faint o'r gloch ydy hi?
    A. Tri phwys
    B. Hanner awr wedi tri
    C. Mae'r gloch yn canu
    D. Tri mochyn bach   0.47

Read the following passage—

Does dim rhaid i mi ddweud wrthych fod Cymru dros ddwy fil o flynyddoedd yn ôl yn wahanol iawn i Gymru heddiw: yn wahanol iawn ei thai a'i hysgolion, ei harferion a'i chwaraeon, fel mai anodd fydd i chi gredu mai yng Nghymru y mae Cynfael, bachgen ein stori, yn byw, mor annhebyg ydy ei fyd o i'ch byd chi.

Dychmygwch yn awr eich bod chi ar ymweliad â Cynfael: y peth cynta y byddwch yn rhyfeddu ato ydy'r tŷ y mae Cynfael yn byw ynddo. Gwelwch nad tŷ o feini neu frics a mortar ydyw, ond tŷ o goed a chlai, a chanddo do o frwyn a grug a brigau mân. Gwelwch y mwg yn codi drwy'r twll yn y tô a'r tân coed sy ar ganol y llawr. Un drws sy i'r tŷ, drws pren ag allwedd haearn i godi'r clicied. O, oes, y mae i'r tŷ ffenestri, ond sylwch mai ffenestri heb wydr ydyn nhw: tyllau yn y wal ydy'r rhain, yn agored y dydd i oleuo'r tŷ, ond yn y nos rhoir darnau o bren drostynt.

Now answer the following questions. Look at the four answers (A,B,C and D) and draw a line under the answer you think is the best.

26. How long ago did Cynfael live in Wales?
    A. two years ago
    B. less than two thousand years ago
    C. more than two thousand years ago
    D. five hundred years ago   0.24

27. How does the writer say you would feel if you saw Cynfael's house?
    A. pleased
    B. surprised

C.   sad

D.   frightened   0.51

28. What was the house built of?

A.   bricks and mortar

B.   stone

C.   wood and clay

D.   canvas   0.25

29. What are we told about the windows?

A.   they were long and narrow

B.   they were closed all day

C.   they had no glass

D.   they were open all night   0.38

30. At night the windows were—

A.   left open

B.   covered with wooden shutters

C.   closed

D.   locked   0.34

31. Which two of the following things were used to make the roof?

A.   slates

B.   twigs

C.   tiles

D.   heather   0.23

32. The writer says Wales was very different when Cynfael lived- 'yn wahanol iawn'. Find another word for 'wahanol' in the passage and write it on the line below.

_____   0.07

In each of the following sentences a word (or two words) is missing. Choose the correct answer (from A,B,C or D) and put a ring around the letter in front of it.

EXAMPLE—

_____ hi yn yr ystafell

A.   Rydw

146

B. Mae
C. Ydy
D. Rydyn

33. _____ e ddim ar y llwyfan
A. Roedd
B. Doeddwn
C. Doedd
D. Roedden   0.24

34. Pwy _____e?
A. oes
B. sy
C. ydy
D. mae   0.43

35. Mae eisiau bwyd _____fe
A. arno
B. arni
C. arna
D. ganddo   0.24

36. _____ chi'n canu yn y côr?
A. Oeddwn
B. Oeddech
C. Oedd
D. Oedden   0.21

37. Rydych chi'n eistedd ar fy _____ i
A. Cap
B. chap
C. nghap
D. gap   0.30

38. _____ i ddim yn ysgrifennu
A. Dydy
B. Dydw
C. Dydyn
D. Rydw   0.24

39. Pwy yw hwn _____?
    A. mae e yma
    B. welais i ddim
    C. sy'n canu'n uchel
    D. y bu yma   0.37

40. Chafodd y plant ddim hyd i'r bêl er _____
    A. maen nhw'n chwilio'n ofalus
    B. mae'r plant wedi chwilio'n ofalus
    C. dydyn nhw ddim wedi chwilio'n ofalus
    D. iddyn nhw chwilio'n ofalus   0.30

We say 'bachgen' for one boy, but 'bechgyn' for more than one.
Write the word for *more than one* of the following things—

41. troed (foot) _____ 0.30
42. llygad (eye) _____ 0.34
43. tŷ (house) _____ 0.18
44. dyn (man) _____ 0.17
45. coeden (tree) _____ 0.55

We say 'merched' for more than one girl, but 'merch' for just
one. Write the word for *one* of the following things—

46. adar (birds) _____ 0.55
47. lloriau (floors) _____ 0.29
48. afonydd (rivers) _____ 0.59
49. defaid (sheep) _____ 0.22
50. ieir (chickens) _____ 0.11

Appendix B.5

Prawf Llafar— sections of an oral test for juniors.

Unit 1
This was the same as the oral test used for infants
(v. Appendix B.3, p.139)

Unit 2
Paired pictures were used in this unit, as in unit 1.
The content of the items was as follows:

Picture 1— words used by tester	Picture 2: expected response
Mae'r bloc hwn yn fach; mae'r bloc hwn yn fawr; mae'r bloc hwn yn fwy; a dyma'r bloc . . .	. . . mwya
Mae'r bachgen hwn yn dew.	Mae'r bachgen hwn yn denau.
Mae'r siocled yn felys; mae'r lemwn yn . . .	. . . sur.
Mae'r bwrdd hwn yn uchel.	Mae'r bwrdd hwn yn isel.
Mae'r ruban hwn yn llydan.	Mae'r ruban hwn yn gul (denau).
Mae'r oen yn wyn fel yr eira.	Mae'r gath yn ddu fel y glo (nos, frân).
Mae'r ferch hon yn llefain (crio)	Mae'r ferch hon yn gwenu (chwerthin).
Mae'r eliffant yn drwm.	Mae'r llygoden yn ysgafn.

Unit 3

One question was asked about each of ten pictures. The picture supplied the answer. Four practice pictures were used in order to train the pupils to reply in complete sentences. The questions and correct answers of the ten test items are given below.

Q. Ydy'r bachgen wedi mynd i gysgu?
A. Ydy, mae'r bachgen wedi mynd i gysgu.

Q. Oes dyn eira yn yr ardd?
A. Oes, mae dyn eira yn yr ardd.

Q. Ydyn nhw'n eistedd yn y cwch?
A. Ydyn, maen nhw'n eistedd yn y cwch.

Q. Oes dillad ar y lein?
A. Nac oes, does dim dillad ar y lein.

Q. Ydyn nhw'n gwisgo capiau?
A. Nac ydyn, dydyn nhw ddim yn gwisgo capiau.

Q. Oes rhywun yn y cae?
A. Nac oes, does neb yn y cae.

Q. Oes rhywbeth yn y bocs?
A. Nac oes, does dim byd yn y bocs.

Q.   Oes llawer o fisgedi ar y plât?
A.   Nac oes, does dim llawer o fisgedi ar y plât.

Q.   Ydy'r doliau yn y gwely?
A.   Ydyn, mae'r doliau yn y gwely.

Q.   Ydy'r ci wedi mynd i gysgu?
A.   Nac ydy, dydy'r ci ddim wedi mynd i gysgu.

Unit 7

The following story was recorded on tape in two versions, one for use in South Wales and one for use in North Wales. While listening to the tape and while re-telling the story, pupils looked at a page of pictures illustrating the story.

— Roedd John yn postio llythyr yn Swyddfa'r Post. Pan oedd e'n sefyll wrth y bocs llythyrau, fe ddaeth dau ddyn i mewn, â 'sanau neilon am eu pennau nhw. Lladron oedden nhw. Fe aeth y lladron at y cownter heb sylwi ar John y tu ôl i'r drws. Fe dynnon' nhw ddrylliau allan o'u pocedi. Fe gododd y clerc ei ddwylo, ac fe aeth y lladron â bagiau o arian. Fe redon' nhw allan o Swyddfa'r Post i'r car. Tra roedden nhw'n neidio i'r car, 'roedd John yn ffonio Swyddfa'r Heddlu.

Cyn iddyn nhw fynd yn bell iawn fe welon' nhw gar yr heddlu ar draws y ffordd, a phlismon â'i law i fyny. Fe droiodd car y lladron i stryd arall. Fe aeth y lladron allan o'r dre tua'r wlad. Ond yn sydyn, dyma nhw'n gweld gwartheg yn blocio'r ffordd o'u blaen nhw. Roedd rhaid stopio.

Tra 'roedden nhw'n aros yng nghanol y gwartheg, fe gyrhaeddodd y plismyn, a mynd â nhw 'nôl i'r ddalfa. Fe ddaeth plismon i ysgwyd llaw gyda John, a diolch iddo fe am ei help.

Appendix C

Analysis of features of the story *(Unit 7*, p.117) appearing in the original version or in pupils' versions of the story.

Feature	Number of pupils who used feature at least once			
	Native speakers	High	Project pupils Average	Low
fe ddaeth	11	1	0	0
fe aeth	7	1	0	0
fe dynnon nhw	4	0	0	0
fe gododd	3	1	0	0
fe redon nhw	3	1	0	0
fe welon nhw	4	0	0	0
fe droiodd	6	0	0	0
fe gyrhaeddodd	0	0	0	0
mae . . . yn	5	12	11	8
mae . . . wedi	3	4	1	0
roedd . . . yn	10	3	0	0
roedd . . . wedi	4	2	1	0
pan	3	4	1	0
tra	3	0	0	0
cyn	4	1	0	0
heb	2	0	0	0
i mewn	11	7	3	0
allan	10	4	3	0
i fyny	7	3	3	0
i lawr	0	4	0	0
tu ôl i	6	3	0	0
wrth	0	2	0	1
yn	4	12	10	4
am	4	1	0	0
i	11	9	10	2
allan o	2	4	2	0
at	5	1	0	0
gyda/hefo/â	8	9	2	0
ar draws	4	1	0	0
tua'r wlad	0	0	0	0
'nôl i	2	1	1	0
ynghanol y	5	0	0	0
ar ôl	2	7	0	0
iddo fe	1	1	0	0
o'u blaen nhw	0	0	0	0
mynd â/gyda	5	2	2	0
arall	9	9	8	0

Appendix D

CONTINGENCY TABLES USED IN CHI-SQUARE TESTS

Categories of scores in *Prawf Gwrando a Deall* related to other variables.

1. *Prawf Gwrando a Deall* x Pupil's sex

		Sex	
		Male	*Female*
Prawf Gwrando	Low	105	91
a Deall scores	Average	116	102
	High	153	160

$x^2 = 1.45$
$d.f = 2$

2. *Prawf Gwrando a Deall* x Socio-economic background

		Socio-economic background				
		1	*2*	*3*	*4*	*5*
Prawf Gwrando	Low	24	38	34	75	22
a Deall scores	Average	31	49	45	74	16
	High	64	55	61	115	15

$x^2 = 15.41$
$d.f. = 8$

3. *Prawf Gwrando a Deall* x Time following Project

		Time following Project			
		1	*2*	*3*	*4*
Prawf Gwrando	Low	19	69	72	25
a Deall scores	Average	14	89	95	14
	High	25	147	128	7

$x^2 = 27.85$
$d.f. = 6$

Prawf Gwrando a Deall scores within category 2 of 'Time following Project' related to two school variables.

4. *Prawf Gwrando a Deall* x Linguistic background

		Linguistic background		
		1	*2*	*3*
Prawf Gwrando	Low	30	21	18
a Deall scores	Average	35	27	26
	High	48	38	61

$x^2 = 6.43$
d.f. $= 4$

5. *Prawf Gwrando a Deall* x Time devoted to Project

		Time devoted to Project		
		1	*2*	*3*
Prawf Gwrando	Low	12	14	43
a Deall scores	Average	4	17	67
	High	0	31	116

$x^2 = 28.98$
d.f. $= 4$

Prawf Gwrando a Deall scores within category 3 of 'Time following Project' related to two school variables.

6. *Prawf Gwrando a Deall* x Linguistic background

		Linguistic background		
		1	*2*	*3*
Prawf Gwrando	Low	25	20	27
a Deall scores	Average	45	24	26
	High	56	43	29

$x^2 = 6.63$
d.f. $= 4$

7. *Prawf Gwrando a Deall* x Time devoted to Project

		Time devoted to Project		
		1	*2*	*3*
Prawf Gwrando	Low	3	35	34
a Deall scores	Average	0	31	64
	High	1	23	104

$x^2 = 28.23$
d.f. $= 4$

Prawf Gwrando a Deall scores related to scores in 2 other tests.

8. *Prawf Gwrando a Deall* x Picture Test A

		Picture Test A		
		Low	Average	High
Prawf Gwrando	Low	5	14	3
a Deall scores	Average	1	16	14
	High	3	30	33

$x^2 = 14.64$
d.f. $= 4$

9. *Prawf Gwrando a Deall* x Reading Test BD

		Reading Test BD		
		Low	Average	High
Prawf Gwrando	Low	6	14	2
a Deall scores	Average	7	20	4
	High	12	34	20

$x^2 = 6.45$
d.f. $= 4$

Categories of scores in *Prawf Llafar* related to other variables

10. *Prawf Llafar* x Pupil's sex

		Sex	
		Male	Female
	Low	29	15
Prawf Llafar scores	Average	29	22
	High	16	24

$x^2 = 5.82$
d.f. $= 2$

11. *Prawf Llafar* x Socio-economic background

		Socio-economic background				
		1	2	3	4	5
	Low	7	11	7	12	7
Prawf Llafar scores	Average	8	14	8	17	3
	High	10	7	4	18	1

$^2 = 9.96$
d.f. $= 8$

12. *Prawf Llafar* x Linguistic background

		Linguistic background		
		1	2	3
Prawf Llafar scores	Low	35	7	2
	Average	41	6	4
	High	21	7	12

$x^2 = 15.55$
d.f. = 4

13. *Prawf Llafar* x Time following Project
(N.B. Only 2 categories of 'Time following Project' represented)

		Time following Project	
		2	3
Prawf Llafar scores	Low	21	22
	Average	23	31
	High	20	22

$x^2 = 0.43$
d.f. = 2

14. *Prawf Llafar* x Time devoted to Project
(N.B. Only 2 categories of 'Time devoted to Project' represented)

		Time devoted to Project	
		2	3
Prawf Llafar scores	Low	25	19
	Average	20	31
	High	13	27

$x^2 = 5.54$
d.f. = 2

Prawf Llafar scores related to scores in 3 other tests.

15. *Prawf Llafar* x *Prawf Gwrando a Deall*

		Prawf Gwrando a Deall		
		Low	Average	High
Prawf Llafar scores	Low	15	20	7
	Average	0	16	32
	High	0	4	34

$x^2 = 59.40$
d.f. = 4

16. *Prawf Llafar* x *Picture Test A*

		Picture Test A		
		Low	Average	High
Prawf Llafar scores	Low	3	20	8
	Average	1	17	18
	High	1	14	19

$x^2 = 7.55$
d.f. $= 4$

17. *Prawf Llafar* x *Reading Test BD*

		Reading Test BD		
		Low	Average	High
Prawf Llafar scores	Low	11	18	2
	Average	7	19	10
	High	5	17	12

$x^2 = 9.60$
d.f. $= 4$

Categories of scores in *Prawf Cymraeg* related to other variables.

The next three tables (18 to 20) were constructed using scores of pupils in schools where Project implementation was not judged to be wholly satisfactory.

18. *Prawf Cymraeg* x Pupil's sex

		Sex	
		Male	Female
Prawf Cymraeg scores	Low	45	39
	Average	46	60
	High	6	16

$x^2 = 5.33$
d.f. $= 2$

19. *Prawf Cymraeg* x Socio-economic background

		Socio-economic background				
		1	2	3	4	5
Prawf Cymraeg scores	Low	8	11	25	30	6
	Average	11	15	32	45	3
	High	7	2	7	4	0

$x^2 = 14.62$
d.f. $= 8$

20. *Prawf Cymraeg* x Linguistic background

		Linguistic background			
		0	*1*	*2*	*3*
	Low	59	9	11	5
Prawf Cymraeg	Average	80	7	8	11
scores	High	7	3	4	8

$x^2 = 23.52$
d.f. $= 6$

The next eight tables (21 to 28) were constructed using scores of pupils in schools where Project implementation was judged to be satisfactory.

21. *Prawf Cymraeg* x Pupil's sex

		Sex	
		Male	*Female*
	Low	32	35
Prawf Cymraeg	Average	41	39
scores	High	24	44

$x^2 = 4.05$
d.f. $= 2$

22. *Prawf Cymraeg* x Socio-economic background

		Socio-economic background				
		1	*2*	*3*	*4*	*5*
	Low	3	13	16	31	2
Prawf Cymraeg	Average	7	17	22	26	7
scores	High	14	14	23	13	2

$x^2 = 20.79$
d.f. $= 8$

23. *Prawf Cymraeg* x Linguistic background

		Linguistic background			
		0	*1*	*2*	*3*
	Low	41	13	7	6
Prawf Cymraeg	Average	57	13	5	5
scores	High	42	9	10	7

$x^2 = 4.86$
d.f. $= 6$

Prawf Cymraeg scores related to scores in 5 other tests.

24.   *Prawf Cymraeg* x *Reading Test BD*

		Reading Test BD		
		Low	*Average*	*High*
	Low	9	8	1
Prawf Cymraeg	Average	10	14	4
scores	High	0	18	17

$x^2 = 26.24$
d.f. $= 4$

25.   *Prawf Cymraeg* x *Maths Test B*

		Maths Test B		
		Low	*Average*	*High*
	Low	9	8	1
Prawf Cymraeg	Average	9	17	2
scores	High	1	26	8

$x^2 = 18.28$
d.f. $= 4$

26.   *Prawf Cymraeg* x *English Progress Test B2*

		English Progress Test B2		
		Low	*Average*	*High*
	Low	9	7	2
Prawf Cymraeg	Average	6	16	6
scores	High	0	12	23

$^2 = 30.66$
d.f. $= 4$

27.   *Prawf Cymraeg* x *Non-verbal Test BD*

		Non-verbal Test BD		
		Low	*Average*	*High*
	Low	9	5	3
Prawf Cymraeg	Average	6	15	7
scores	High	0	22	13

$x^2 = 21.44$
d.f. $= 4$

28. *Prawf Cymraeg* x *Verbal Test BC*

| | Verbal Test BC | | |
	Low	*Average*	*High*
Low	10	7	1
Average	9	14	5
High	1	15	19

$\chi^2 = 26.16$
d.f. $= 4$

Schools Council Project on Bilingual Education (Secondary Schools) 1974-1978: Methodology

C. J. Dodson

THE AIM OF THE PROJECT was to initiate a feasibility study of a communicatively orientated language-learning programme at secondary-school level and to produce a range of appropriate experimental materials and resources. The purpose of this paper is to describe the tested methodology and to explain how materials and resources were used.

The Project was originally intended for children from the Schools Council Bilingual Education Primary School Project so as to establish a continuing bilingual education for these children from the age of 5 into the first three years of secondary schools, where English is still the medium of instruction for all subjects and where Welsh is offered on the basis of a one-hour lesson per day. However, the intakes into our growing number of English-medium comprehensive schools come from wide catchment areas representing a broad spectrum of primary schools ranging from those who produce children who have become fully bilingual by the age of eleven to those outside the Schools Council Primary Scheme where for various reasons the children move into the comprehensive school with little or no Welsh. All these children with different levels of proficiency as well as different levels of ability might find themselves in the same secondary-school class. It was for this reason that all printed-word materials for pupils were written in three language-categories reflecting different levels of difficulty, and teachers were thus able to select categories appropriate to the needs of their children, either in different classes or within the same class.

As the Project was a communicatively orientated programme, the materials and resources needed were totally different from traditional language course books. Although the three language categories reflected a rough grading of speech patterns in terms of grammatical complexity, the main focus of the total programme related to the communicative needs of the children. If true com-

161

municative interactions are to take place in the classroom right from the beginning of the course, learners cannot be held to a strict grammatical progression which might postpone a speech pattern of high communicative frequency for several years when it is in fact needed in the first few weeks. Two typical examples are interactions which require a past tense or the subjunctive.

COMMUNICATIVE INTERACTIONS IN THE CLASSROOM

All interactions in the classroom, no matter whether between teacher and pupil or between pupil and pupil, are communication of one kind or another. Yet there are two main levels of communication in classroom interactions, and although both are vital in the foreign/second language-learning process only one of these levels gives pupils a real opportunity to reach communicative competence. Observations of language teaching through single lessons, not only in Wales but in classes seen in many countries throughout the world, show quite clearly that normal classroom interactions fall mainly into one of the lower communicative levels and the process does not often progress into the higher communicative levels where communicative competence can flourish. Hence many teachers are faced with the constant struggle of creating classroom situations which despite extreme efforts by all concerned do not bring their pupils to a stage where they can handle language in truly communicative acts. This state of affairs has, of course, great implications for bilingual countries where attempts are being made to make originally monoglot speakers sufficiently bilingual to cope with everyday life in the second language outside school.

In the lower levels of communication, generally the only type to be found in most classrooms, the attention of teachers' and pupils' minds is focused mainly on the language itself. No matter whether teacher or pupil presents the stimulus, the underlying speech intention is to discover whether someone is able to make a linguistic response and if so, whether this response is correct or incorrect. The focus is on the form rather than the content, on the medium rather than the message. Hence this type of communication is called *medium-orientated communication.*

Whilst medium-orientated communication is a vital activity in every lesson cycle for any topic, it cannot by itself give pupils an opportunity to develop communicative competence. It is therefore important for teachers to create classroom interactions where the focus of pupils' minds is on the transmission of messages which are not about the language-learning process but which are made to satisfy immediate non-linguistic needs such as satisfying curiosity,

resolving uncertainty,expressing opinions, agreements and contradictions, making more predictable the less predictable, acquiring
knowledge and a host of other needs felt by all pupils. This type of
classroom interaction is called *message-orientated communication.*

Teachers are, therefore, advised to make a distinction between
pupils' merely *using* language (to show the teacher that they can use
it) and *making use of* language, a type of communication in which
language has become a tool or vehicle and not an end in itself. In
any lesson cycle relating to a topic or unit, both these types of
communication will occur, though the aim is to move from the
lower to the higher levels.

It should not be assumed however, that only medium-orientated
communication should feature for the first few months at the
beginning of the course in order to prepare pupils for later message-
orientated communication. Both types of communication should
occur right from the beginning of the course, with teachers and
pupils trying to communicate for constantly lengthening periods at
message-orientated levels as the weeks and months progress.

On the other hand, teachers should not fall into the trap of
forcing message-orientated communication onto pupils who are
not yet ready for this type of interaction for a given topic because
they lack the practice at medium-orientated levels, which should
have preceded each switching to message-orientated levels in every
lesson or lesson cycle. The process should be one of constant
fluctuation between the two main levels, with both teachers and
pupils trying to communicate whenever appropriate at the higher
levels.

In general classroom procedures these two types of communication are not 'either-or' processes, where in one minute pupils
communicate at the medium-orientated level and in the next they
are communicating on a fully message-orientated level. In practice
these two types of communication should be seen as extreme poles
on a continuum where, in the development towards message-
orientated communication in any lesson cycle, there are mixtures of
both forms in varying degrees. Nevertheless, the constant aim of
the teacher is to give the pupil an opportunity to lose himself in the
content (the message) of the materials and to become less and less
aware of the linguistic utterances he makes to satisfy the immediate
non-linguistic needs generated in him by the materials, resources
and classroom activities.

MATERIALS AND RESOURCES
If language-learning is to become a truly communicative activity

it is clear that the interactions which take place in a class are unique to that class, especially as one of the main characteristics of message-orientated communication is the high degree of unpredictability of content in the utterances made by pupils during any interaction. Each individual in the classroom, whether pupil or teacher, brings with him a whole spectrum of unique pre-perceptions about the items and topics to be tackled.

It is therefore important to realise that the materials used in the Project were not in the form of the traditional textbook, which almost invariably holds both teachers and pupils locked in medium-orientated communication. Moreover, teachers and pupils had to supply additional materials to those supplied by Project Officers, since each individual within each class brings his own particular needs and interests to be shared with others through the medium of Welsh.

For language work at medium-orientated levels, every unit requires a basic situational dialogue reflecting the language used in normal communicative interactions which pupils will encounter both in and out of school. These dialogues are the main linguistic input for the class as a whole in any lesson cycle and should consist of an appropriate number of utterances for between three and five characters. During message-orientated communication there will be opportunities for further linguistic inputs, but these relate to the specific, and often unpredictable, needs of individual pupils and not to the class as a whole.

There is no limit to the collection of appropriate materials and resources suitable for truly message-orientated interactions. Apart from printed-word materials, sources can range from items in Sunday supplements, personal snapshots, models made at home, items collected from visits abroad, and equipment, charts, apparatus, models, etc., some of which may originally have been intended for other school subjects and be now lying forgotten in some storeroom, but which can once more be put to good use in the language lesson, depending on the topic being dealt with at the time. Even the teachers of other subjects, if they are Welsh-speakers, may be persuaded to pay short visits now and again to the 'language' lesson if they have a free period, and add their own point of view and expertise to the interactions taking place. These 'guests' must of course be briefed by the language teacher about the language proficiency levels of the particular class.

In many ways this new approach changes the role of the language teacher. He is no longer merely a teacher of language, but ultimately a teacher of something else, where language has become a tool or vehicle for communication. Indeed, in many instances he is no longer even 'the teacher', but has become a mere participant in a communicative act. In the final analysis, the second language ceases to be the ultimate or only objective of the lesson, an end in itself, with the pupils having to find their own second-language message-orientated interactions as best they may outside the school.

At the beginning of the Project some language teachers felt a little uncertain in their new role. As a consequence, the materials included reference- and data-sheets to help them with any subject information they might require. Nobody expects the language teacher to know everything about everything. In fact, *not* knowing certain data is a good opportunity for message-orientated communication between pupils and teachers. It has already been stated that one of the main characteristics of message-orientated interaction is its unpredictability; the fact that the teacher on occasions genuinely has to ask for information, and hence will receive unpredictable answers, should not be considered as unusual or in some way wrong, but as an excellent opportunity to generate real conversation. Even during medium-orientated language work conditions for message-orientated communication may arise. Here the occasion as well as the content will be unpredictable, but again the teacher must not be frightened to grasp those 'fleeting moments of opportunity' to engage in a truly message-orientated interaction before the requirements of the lesson demand a return to medium-orientated work.

To help teachers further, the materials and resources, both printed-word, pictorial and non-print, were divided into a number of major *fields of interest,* each of which was sub-divided into various *topics* relating to curricular and extra-curricular areas. The printed-word language materials were presented throughout at three different levels of language difficulty.

For both content and language, therefore, the teachers were able to exercise a great deal of flexibility, according to the needs and interests of their pupils; a teacher could, if he so wished, tackle consecutively the various topics from a given field of interest, e.g. Space Science, or he could select one topic, such as Design or Communication and follow it across several fields of interest, e.g. Space Science, Red Indians, Paper. All options and choices open to the class depended on the degree of interest shown by the pupils in any topic or field of interest.

At the same time, the teacher could select the *language category* appropriate to the proficiency level of his pupils. It should be noted that in a communicatively based language programme it is the frequency of the communicative acts normally occurring in the outside world that governs the progression of teaching and learning, and not the traditional grammatical progression from simple to more complex speech patterns or structures, found hitherto in our textbooks. Communicative interactions which are functionally extremely basic and necessary in normal communication, and hence of high frequency, may include speech patterns which would be postponed if language teaching were based on a traditional grammatical progression. In our system these patterns cannot be ignored or postponed. Pupils learn these complex sentences as a single 'one-off' unit, to be used only in the context of the particular situation taught at the time. At a later stage, when pupils are ready, the more complex sentence structures can be used in substitution and manipulation exercises during appropriate medium-orientated communication.

However, alternative speech patterns are normally available for executing high-frequency communicative acts in the target language. The teacher, therefore, should be able to select patterns of a linguistic complexity suitable for the proficiency of his pupils at any given time. Should patterns of a required degree of complexity (or simplicity) not be available, it is suggested that the progression relating to the frequency order of communicative acts should take priority over purely grammatical progression, and patterns falling outside the proficiency level of pupils at a given stage should be included and used as described above.

METHODOLOGY

The method tested during the lifetime of the Project and found to be successful in helping learners to pass through medium-orientated communication to message-orientated communication for any topic, can be represented in a simple diagram:

The learning sequences shown in the above diagram represent a full lesson-cycle of between six and twelve or more lessons, depending on the amount of materials and resources to be used, the complexity of the subject and the interest shown by pupils in the topic.

In the space available here, only a broad outline of the various steps can be given. For more detailed information, please refer to the books and articles quoted at the end of this paper.

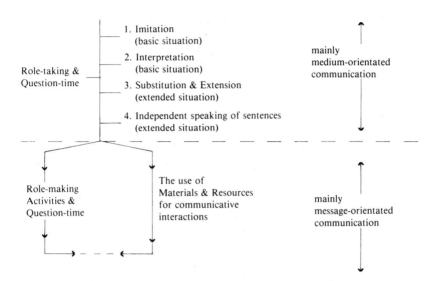

IMITATION (*Step 1*)

Use as your basic situation a dialogue appropriate for your chosen topic. The purpose of this drill exercise (medium-orientated) is for the pupils to learn how to speak fluently and accurately the sentences, or rather, utterances of the dialogue. Give the meanings of the Welsh utterances using your spoken model as their cue. Please ensure that in addition to acquiring a good pronunciation and a fluent delivery, the pupils learn to use the correct intonation. The exercise should develop quickly and rhythmically, with the teacher selecting pupils at random. Since this activity is extremely intense, do not continue with it for more than ten minutes unless you are certain that your pupils are capable of longer periods. Picture cues, e.g. picture strips, will help pupils to retain the meanings which were given by the teacher as the new utterance was introduced. The printed text of the dialogue should be available for the pupils to scan whilst they are listening to the utterances, but pupils should look away, either at you or at the relevant picture, when they are making a response. This ensures that your spoken model is the primary stimulus, whilst the printed word remains a secondary stimulus. Used in this way, the printed word enhances the pupils' imitation performance rather than interferes with it.

INTERPRETATION (*Step 2*)

Although the teacher has given the mother-tongue equivalents of the sentences practised in *Step 1,* some pupils will have forgotten the meanings by the end of the imitation work. One of the purposes of interpretation work is to consolidate the meaning of the Welsh sentences. Furthermore this is the first opportunity for pupils to learn how to switch rapidly from one language to the other, and how to keep them apart, important factors in bilingual education. Pupils must also learn to say a Welsh utterance without having heard the teacher's Welsh model immediately beforehand.

The procedure is for the teacher to say the English equivalents of utterances in the basic situation practised in *Step 1,* whilst requiring from the pupils an immediate interpretation in Welsh. If a pupil cannot make an immediate, correct, response, the teacher switches to another pupil; if the latter succeeds, the teacher returns to the first pupil. The ten-minute rule once more applies, despite the fact that pupils may greatly enjoy this work, especially when they see how efficient they are as interpreters.

These two steps should have allowed most pupils to learn how to speak fluently and accurately the utterances of the basic dialogue. Yet communication is more than the mere ability to speak utterances. True communication consists of three interactional elements: verbal, paralinguistic and non-verbal. It is therefore important for pupils to be given the opportunity to learn how to cope also with paralinguistic and non-verbal interactions. Para-linguistic interactions are the sounds made by participants to transmit a message without actually using words. The most common sounds are *Ah!*, *Oh!*(?), *Mm!*(?), usually uttered with a great deal of intonation and stress. Non-verbal interactions consist of a whole range of body language involving gestures and facial expressions. More than one element is brought into play in most communicative acts. For instance, the verbal message 'I don't know' is usually combined with a slight shaking of the head or shrugging of the shoulders, agreement may involve nodding, with or without the use of words or grunts, and hesitation is often indicated paralinguistically ('Er . . .'), together with some sort of body language. All these behaviour patterns have to be fused with purely verbal utterances in a communicatively orientated pro-gramme. During imitation and interpretation work (*Steps 1* and *2*), the pupils remained seated in their desks, a position which hinders any development leading to the fusion of verbal, paralinguistic and non-verbal communicative behaviour. It is therefore vital for pupils to be given an opportunity at this stage to practise the more sophisticated communicative skills through role-taking.

ROLE-TAKING

Role-taking is to be distinguished from role-making. In role-taking pupils act out the dialogue learnt in *Steps 1* and *2*. In other words, pupils 'take' the roles already supplied and are not required at this stage to create their own roles as demanded by role-making activities. As the pupils are still *practising* the three elements of communication, role-taking is medium-orientated unless some pupils can lose themselves in a role as some actors can on stage. Role-taking would then be partly medium- and partly message-orientated.

Groups of three, four or five pupils, depending on the number of characters in the playlet, are required to perform the playlet in front of the class who act as audience. Proper stage props are not a vital requirement, as often items found in classrooms can be used as substitutes.

As the playlets can be acted out in a couple of minutes or so, it is possible to give most if not all the groups an opportunity to perform. Each performance should be rewarded by appropriate applause from the audience.

Please note that although pupils were able to say the sentences of the dialogue fluently and accurately whilst sitting in their desks, many of them will no longer have the same *linguistic* competence now that for the first time they have to combine words with actions. This shows quite clearly that during traditional language teaching, a teacher can easily be fooled into thinking that his pupils are fluent and accurate, yet once they are freed from his linguistic control and are required to apply language in normal communicative situations, he may find that they have not after all reached the necessary level of automatic response. Thus sufficient practice in role-play is vital in language learning if we wish our pupils to develop a level of communicative competence to satisfy bilingual requirements.

Each performance is followed by Question-Time.

QUESTION-TIME

After each group has completed a role-taking activity and has received the appropriate applause, the audience is invited to put questions in Welsh about the playlet to the individual performers, who are still in front of the class. The performers of course answer in Welsh. Experience has shown that some members of the audience will put questions in the hope that the performers will not have an immediate, or indeed any, answer available, from the point of view not of language but of content. In this activity, language

169

can thus become secondary, a tool or vehicle to communicate messages, and to the extent that the speech intentions of the participants relate to content rather than form, the interactions have become message-orientated. This is the first opportunity in a lesson cycle for pupils to be able to participate in message-orientated communication although everything depends as always on the speech intentions of pupils and teachers. Are the participants interested more in the language at the moment of making an utterance, or in sending a message? The more the focus remains on language, the more the interaction will remain medium-orientated. Focus on language is of course a vital prerequisite for reaching message-orientated communication in any lesson cycle, but it will by itself never afford pupils a chance to reach communicative competence. In addition, the language items learnt will not 'stick' and will have to be retaught tomorrow, next week or even next year.

A large number of pupils will seek clarification about the playlet, although in role-taking the degree of unpredictability and uncertainty relating to content is not very great. The less gifted pupils will often resort to stereotyped questions which can be put for almost every playlet, e.g. 'What time (day) was it when you . . .?' or 'Does your mother (father, sister, etc.) know that you . . .?', or 'How old are you?', if one of the characters seems to be an elderly person. Although teachers should encourage the audience to put more adventurous questions as time progresses, stereotyped questions should not be taken amiss or rejected. They reflect real-life communication where individuals make simple utterances in order not to be left out of the game. The main point of question-time is that it produces spontaneous and unpredictable exchanges, and even stereotyped questions can achieve this at times.

As in role-taking, children will make more *linguistic* errors during question-time than under tightly-controlled teacher-directed medium-orientated communication. During these message-orientated exchanges, teachers should resist the temptation to correct every error made by pupils, as this destroys the very thing they are trying to create, namely a message-orientated interaction. The teacher should, however, note the errors made and spend time correcting them after the exchanges have ceased. At that point, the lesson has once more switched down to medium-orientated communication. The points of difficulty should then be incorporated in future dialogues and playlets in the hope that some linguistic errors will not be repeated. Many of them *will* be repeated, no matter how intensely the correct form has been drilled. The pressure of the communicative event tends to distort apparently fully automatised utterances and it is a matter of time and application for these linguistic errors to disappear.

Up to this stage in the lesson cycle teachers and pupils have dealt merely with the basic situation, in the main through medium-orientated communication but also through message-orientated communication in varying degrees during question-time.

Learning to speak and act out a series of basic situations, however, is only a part of language learning, though absolutely vital in the development towards communicative competence. What is required now is for pupils to learn, through substitution and extension work, how to manipulate linguistically the utterances they can already speak fluently and accurately in a communicative setting. They will thus be able to create new utterances with new meanings though still using known vocabulary and speech patterns or structures.

SUBSTITUTION AND EXTENSION (*Step 3*)

The teacher takes the utterances of the basic playlet and interchanges words or sentence elements with words or elements which occurred elsewhere in the playlet or in previous playlets. He then presents the mother-tongue version of these new sentences to individual pupils and requires an immediate Welsh version. For example, 'It's too hot to play football' can be changed to 'It's too wet to play football (cricket, etc.)' if the words 'wet' or 'cricket' occur in the same playlet or have been used in previous playlets.

The weaker pupil can usually cope with the substitution of only one word or element. Elements usually consist of phrases such as 'to go swimming', thus a substitution might change from 'It's too cold to play football' to 'It's too cold to go swimming', if the inserted element has occurred previously.

Teachers will often find that the Welsh-language response from the pupil is so quick that they are not immediately ready with their next mother-tongue stimulus. Some teachers may wish to prepare for themselves a list of utterances with substituted elements so that they will not be caught out. After a few weeks, however, most teachers are sufficiently flexible and nimble of mind to think rapidly of a whole range of new utterances.

The *extension* work of this activity consists of stringing together two or more clauses or utterances. This is especially important at the beginning of a course, when utterances in the basic situation are normally crisp and short, since pupils need to learn from the very start how to speak and act out longer utterances it they are to cope with language in the true sense. High frequency conjunctions such as 'and' and 'but' should be taught, if not already learnt in the basic dialogue, and used to stitch together two or more clauses.

Although in *Steps 2* and *3* the teacher uses the pupils' mother-tongue as a cue for an immediate Welsh response, the pupils are not translating word for word in this process, or else they would never be able to make an *immediate* response. They are transposing concepts, conjured up by the teacher's cue. It is the concept and the related Welsh utterance that are in the pupil's mind during his response, and not the mother-tongue words spoken previously by the teacher. It is in fact the same operation a highly skilled simultaneous interpreter performs when giving an immediate inter-pretation of somebody else's speech.

Whereas in both steps the teacher produces the concepts and the pupils create the language, linguistically *Step 3* is a semi-creative process since the pupils generate utterances they have never spoken or heard before, and this ability is vital if they wish to make use of language to satisfy a wide range of unpredictable events. Merely knowing parrot-fashion the utterances of the basic situation is of little use to pupils, especially in a bilingual situation.

Step 3 is, therefore, the first attempt in every lesson cycle to break out of the basic situation so as to be able to create new situations in later steps. However, without the *linguistic* skill of manipulating known utterances, pupils will never be able to take part in *communicative* acts which by their very nature are un-predictable and free of controls.

Teachers should, therefore, begin to chain their substitution and extension cues in terms of related meanings so that not only are new utterances being produced in isolation, but pupils are speaking related utterance chains which express new situations.

Nevertheless, because in *Step 3* the focus is on language, it is a medium-orientated communicative activity. We are still 'using' language and not 'making use' of it as a tool to satisfy an immediate non-linguistic need, as was the case to a greater or lesser extent during question-time after role-taking. Pupils, however, are now ready to make utterances free of control though not to bear the pressure of a full communicative act.

INDEPENDENT SPEAKING OF SENTENCES (*Step 4*)
In this step pupils are asked to speak any Welsh utterance, whether statement or question, from the basic situation or those generated in *Step 3*. They are then encouraged to speak any two, three or more utterances that come to their minds. They are then asked to

produce a series of utterances which are related in terms of meaning, so that part-situations are being generated. Gradually pupils become able to produce longer and longer utterance chains so that they are in fact relating a total event. Under experimental conditions some pupils in the third month of their course were observed to speak for twenty minutes or more without repeating themselves.

In this activity motivation is extremely high and before long pupils begin to direct one of their utterances at the teacher or another pupil who must continue the chaining before directing an utterance at another participant. In this process the interchanges are often transformed into true communicative interactions, although pupils still remain seated in their desks. Content becomes more important than form, and message-orientated communication takes place, before one of the subsequent speakers drops down again to medium-orientated communication by focusing on the language.

Step 4 is thus a watershed between medium and message-orientated communication and pupils are now ready linguistically to participate fully in communicative acts.

ROLE-MAKING

All activities from now on in the lesson cycle become progressively more message-orientated. Role-making can be divided into four phases:

a) In role-taking after *Step 2* pupils began to learn how to combine verbal with paralinguistic and non-verbal behaviour. At that stage, however, they were not required to create the situation of the playlet as they would not have been linguistically ready for such work. At the end of *Step 4*, however, they have had sufficient practice in the basic situation and its linguistic and conceptual extensions (*Steps 3* and *4*) to start creating their own situations in playlet form. As with all other aspects in education, the development of pupils' ability to create new playlets and participate in role-making is gradual. In phase a) pupils are merely required to substitute words and utterance elements in the basic situation so as to create a new situation which, however, is still closely related in content to the original situation.

For the preparation of playlets pupils divide up into small groups, depending on the number of characters required by the playlets, and disperse to different parts of the classroom. Some pupils sit in or on their desks, others prefer to stand. The noise level is of necessity higher than in lessons of other subjects, but then so is the work intensity. In any case, language lessons conducted in comparative silence would seem a contradiction in terms. The main thing to remember is that the teacher is still in complete control of the classroom situation.

At this stage the teacher's role is to assist his pupils in their preparation work. He should also have helped select the groups in the first place, particularly if he wishes to set group homework which will require members of a group to live near each other.

As he visits the various groups he will frequently be asked for new words and phrases. At times pupils will overreach themselves linguistically and the teacher will have to dissuade them from using particular phrases. He has to act as a judge in these situations, trying to find a compromise between the pupils' desire to create an original situation and their linguistic limitations. The old dictum 'If you can't say it, change it or drop it' would seem appropriate here.

In this preparation work, Project pupils initially used English freely, e.g. ' "Edrych ar y ddaear!" Armstrong looks through the porthole and says, "O! Ie. O! Welaist ti rywbeth yn debyg erioed? Gwych bachan!" '* As the Project progressed, less and less English was used by pupils in setting up their playlets.

Almost all pupils wrote down their own lines whilst many also wrote down the lines of their fellow-players. This was in contrast to German pupils in a parallel experiment for the learning of English as a foreign language in Germany, where only some wrote down their own lines and hardly any wrote the lines of their co-players (Butzkamm/Dodson: 1980). Could the reason for this be that classroom language-learning in British schools is still so heavily biased towards writing rather than speaking? In this case, however, the pupils who write down their own and others' lines might well be at an advantage, as the sequencing of a playlet is often forgotten after a week or so by the players themselves if no written record exists.

When the groups have completed their new playlets, usually after approximately ten minutes, each group performs its playlet in front of the class. Every performance is followed again by Question-Time which is now far more message-orientated than the exchanges made after role-taking, since every performance is less predictable and produces more items of curiosity, with no group knowing anything about the content of the playlets created by any of the other groups.

* i.e. 'Look at the earth!' 'Oh! Yes. Oh! Did you ever see anything like it? Great, lad!'

b) In the second phase of role-making, the groups are encouraged to combine and re-combine previously performed playlets so as to produce new and/or extended playlets. The combinations involved are varied and points of connection occur in different places for different groups. Preparation time is by now greatly reduced as pupils become more proficient in both the use of their imaginations and their ability to express new combinations of ideas. During performances the groups really have to try to communicate with their audiences, since every playlet is seen and heard for the first time by the audience at the time of the performance. For instance, items from basic situations 'Having breakfast' and 'A day out' might be re-combined by a group and moulded into a playlet dealing with 'A picnic by the river', which has never been dealt with by the class. Question-time after these performances can become heated affairs with frequent contradictions and differences of opinion. This is of course true message-orientated communication in what is usually described as the 'artificial' environment of the language classroom. Clearly there is nothing artificial in the way these pupils make use of the second language. Language here is not an end in itself; the message is the important factor, with the second language acting merely as a tool in the pupils' desire to satisfy their curiosity, make their point or resolve uncertainties.

The impression should not be given that there is a long time gap between phases a) and b). We are not talking here about pupils' development from one year to the next or even of the postponement of phase b) for a term or so. Phase b) can be introduced as soon as the pupils have mastered a small number of topics. The ability of pupils to handle phase b) activities does not depend on the range of language acquired but on the pupils' ability to permutate and manipulate utterance elements in a classroom milieu which has encouraged the transmission of genuine messages.

c) This phase is called *spontaneous* role-making. Pupils or teacher throw out a title to the group of pupils in front of the class who are required to invent *and* perform an appropriate playlet on the spot without prior preparation. The group could also be asked to perform so-called 'actional roles', such as purchaser, negotiator or doctor's patient, roles which occur in the course of our active lives (Littlewood, 1975), no matter whether connected with the Project topics or not.

Teachers need not break their hearts if their pupils are incapable of spontaneous role-making at the beginning of the course. In the German feasibility studies the pupils, who were raw beginners, were able to cope with spontaneous role-making by the end of their first year. Welsh pupils in the Schools Council Project were able to handle this communicative situation sooner, but then all of them had learnt some Welsh at primary school. Some had even been role-making before reaching secondary school.

d) The aim of this phase is to take role-making outside the classroom. First of all the teacher should communicate in Welsh with his pupils outside the classroom on school premises. If there are any communicative interactions which seem to recur time and again outside the classroom, weave these interactions into your own basic dialogues so that the various interactions can be played out in the classroom. This additional competence will give both teacher and pupil a far greater incentive to communicate in Welsh outside the classroom and make pupils more aware of the reality of the Welsh language, should this be needed by the pupils. Indeed, the basic situations should include any interactions occuring outside the school altogether which you believe appropriate for the pupils in your area to tackle through the medium of Welsh.

An additional avenue would be for the teacher to contact sympathetic Welsh-speakers who normally deal with your pupils outside school through the medium of English. Local shopkeepers, disc-jockeys or even Ministers of Religion spring readily to mind. A Welsh-speaking owner of the school tuck-shop would present a marvellous opportunity for the pupils to make real use of Welsh once the normal 'tuck-shop interactions' had been developed to message-orientated level in the classroom. Furthermore it would do nothing but good if the owner of the tuck-shop were invited to one of the lessons with some of his ware to participate in real communicative acts through the medium of Welsh. Indeed, it would be sound practice, not only linguistically but educationally, to extend invitations to a whole range of potential visitors in the community, since the gap between Welsh in school and Welsh in the street, even between school itself and the community at large, could be more readily bridged by such activities.

THE USE OF MATERIALS AND RESOURCES

The diagram on page 167 showed two avenues which, when combined, lead to bilingual education. One avenue was via role-making as described above, the other is via the use of materials and resources.

Once the pupils are able to handle the second language at a message-orientated level in relation to some of the vocabulary and structures needed to deal with areas of knowledge related to e.g.

'Space' and 'Space Science', the appropriate materials and resources prepared for this topic can be used for classroom interactions. The purpose of this procedure is once more to give pupils an opportunity to focus their minds on something other than language, and at the same time deal with areas which are educationally desirable or necessary. It is at this stage that teachers and pupils can bring a whole range of their own materials into the classroom.

It may well be that some pupils know more about the subject area than does the teacher, as some young people are almost obsessed with their particular interests. This is all to the good in our classroom situation, for these pupils will be particularly eager to share their knowledge with others, especially if they can reinforce the transmission of their knowledge with their own aids and resources. The interactions to satisfy this desire are obviously message-orientated, although from time to time the teacher may have to supply the occasional word or phrase which the pupil considers to be vital in his endeavour to show both teachers and pupils what he knows about the subject.

Even if on most occasions the teacher has a greater knowledge of the topic, the whole process should be seen in broad terms as one of discovery, in which everyone attempts to make his own contribution.

It is also possible to use a narrative as a basic situation and practice the sentences of the piece through the initial four steps at medium-orientated levels, in this case omitting role-taking after *Step 2* but using the materials and resources as before, at message-orientated levels.

It should be obvious that a vast range of commercial materials and resources, especially if supplemented by his own aids, allow the teacher to introduce project work where all the pupils are involved in some capacity, but where all the interactions can now be made through the medium of Welsh.

It is important to remember that pupils' interests change from one year to the next depending on fashion or the particular topics on which the media, especially television, are concentrating at any given time. It is here that pupils can help to supplement materials, so that the focus of the lesson is on topics which are up-to-date and truly relevant to the young person.

It is also possible for pupils to supply the ideas for their own basic situations, for which the teacher will help to supply the appropriate language. In this way, basic situations can be closely related to any new interests which his class might show in any area of knowledge. The greater the interest, the more pupils and teacher are pulled towards message-orientated communication in the classroom.

Many of these fields of knowledge lie within curricular areas. It might, therefore, be profitable to involve sympathetic, but thoroughly briefed, Welsh-speaking teachers of other subjects to spend the occasional ten minutes or so in the Welsh lessons. These teachers are able to extend the pupils' interests and supply valuable additional information because of their own superior specialised knowledge of the subject.

In all these procedures the communicative aim is for Welsh to become a relevant vehicle for the transmission of knowledge. Welsh will have become a normal ingredient in tasks which have nothing to do with the Welsh language itself. But that is precisely the role which any living language plays in the daily lives of individuals.

The educational advantages in a wider sense should also be obvious. The pupils' Welsh is being used to widen their educational horizons, and most teachers of other subjects are only too glad to see their own subjects reinforced in the so-called 'language lesson'. Linguistically Welsh is being strengthened from day to day. Most important of all the language will become real to the learners and not be considered as some abstract code to be learnt for its own sake or merely for some distant examination.

Models brought by pupils are also a good tool for making real use of language, especially if the relevant vocabulary and structures have been fused into basic situations and learnt through medium-orientated levels prior to close examination of the design and functions of the models. Actually making the models in class is another rich source for communicative acts. Utterances such as 'Where's the glue?' or 'Pass me the scissors!' do not occur in our textbooks. Yet these sentences are part of the ordinary language heard every day in every school throughout the country.

Through the making of models, the Welsh lesson is clearly on the way to becoming an Arts and Crafts lesson through the medium of Welsh, and other school subjects such as Physical Education and Art could also be partially woven into the time set aside for Welsh lessons. However, all this work cannot be carried out successfully on an ad hoc basis. Everything has to be carefully planned, appropriate basic situations have to be made, and disciplined (though enjoyable) medium-orientated work has to be followed through in order to reach what at any rate most of the Project teachers felt to be the real pleasures of language teaching, namely making use of Welsh in true communicative acts in areas of extreme interest to both teacher and pupil.

Not only are these activities the first steps in leading pupils towards bilingual education; this approach is also seriously being considered in many parts of the world as the only way out of the frustration of teaching a foreign or second language for periods of up to ten years with little visible success despite all the effort, time and money spent in the process.

Apart from model-making materials, teachers should also make available games and quizzes for classroom use. Some may consider these items as light relief, or the sugar on the pill, but if these items are seen in the context of the above method, it should be clear that they are nothing of the kind in the second-language development of the learner. In order to execute the activity or play the game, the pupil has to apply language, no matter whether at medium or at message-orientated levels although our constant striving is for the medium not to remain the message. In most of our language lessons, the medium *is* the message and this is precisely the obstacle which has prevented us for so long from giving our pupils a chance to become communicatively competent. A distinction must be made between teaching language and teaching communication. Teaching language is a part, perhaps the major part, of teaching communication, but without switching the pupil from the medium to the message we shall 'tread water' forever.

This approach is even more important for bilingual countries, or more precisely for countries who wish to maintain, or even extend, bilingualism. Wales is just such a country, and as language teachers we should re-examine our roles in the language-teaching process. New insights and attitudes are required to help Welshmen regain and retain, their professed identity.

No one assumes that the school can solve all linguistic and communicative problems as far as Welsh is concerned. The world outside the school perhaps bears a greater responsibility. The teacher may be very successful in developing in his pupils a high degree of communicative competence in Welsh, but if the outside world does not wish to communicate with his pupils through the medium of Welsh, he could be forgiven for questioning the value of all his efforts, expertise and professionalism. It is therefore, important, to involve outsiders in your lessons, as described above, so as to throw bridges between the smaller community of the school and the wider world outside.

First of all, however, we have to show the outside world that we can be highly successful in teaching a second language, and this requires new approaches. In supplying a range of materials and resources for several major fields of interest, consisting of factual, narrative, fictional and instructional materials, also dialogues, playlets, games, quizzes, crosswords, miscellaneous visual aids and models, together with teachers' notes, resources and commercial addresses for obtaining additional resources, the Project gave participating teachers and pupils an opportunity to adjust themselves to a communicative approach. It is hoped that other agencies, governmental or commercial, will take over this role. Nevertheless, teachers must at the same time show that they are prepared to adopt new ways of teaching.

READING AND WRITING

All the activities described so far relate to communicative behaviour mainly focused on understanding and speaking. The printed word in the form of the printed basic situation has already been introduced during *Step 1*. Once a few further steps have been completed in any lesson cycle, narratives can be used for reading purposes. Here, as in other communicative acts, the learner can operate at two main levels. Is the pupil reading in order to learn how to read in Welsh, or is he reading something in Welsh in order to know what it says because he is interested in the content? Once again the teacher gently weans the pupil away from the medium to the message as the lesson cycle progresses. The school library now comes into play, so as to satisfy the various needs of every individual in the class. The cooperation of the school librarian and the County Library Service should be gained so that pupils may be supplied with any relevant Welsh-medium reading materials which are available.

Writing work too should be introduced at the beginning of the course and not be postponed for a term or more. Once again we operate at two main levels. At the medium-orientated level pupils write in order to learn to spell correctly what they can already say correctly. Dictation work is an extremely important exercise in this respect. Pupils may even write essays, reports, dialogues and playlets. At first they may do so merely to show the teacher their linguistic competence, i.e. the *medium* is still the 'message'. However, the pupils must be switched as soon as appropriate in any lesson cycle to writing something in Welsh in order to transmit true messages to someone else, whether another pupil, the teacher or a penfriend who may live many miles away. Everything depends on the ultimate intention of the writing act.

Project work, described earlier, in which pupils attempt to discover what to them is new knowledge, presents a large number of opportunities for pupils to lift the various writing aspects mentioned above, e.g. reports, descriptions, opinions, arguments, essays, letters, preparation of booklets including visual and statistical data, from a medium to a message-orientated level, because the content of project work is interesting and important to the pupils.

The teacher is the only person able to decide the amount of time to be devoted to the various communicative skills. He alone can accomplish the fine tuning required to help his individual pupils to develop gradually from knowing nothing about a particular basic situation to being able by the end of the lesson cycle to handle competently the various communicative demands found in the real world in relation to that particular topic.

TESTS AND EXAMINATIONS

Tests and examinations are medium-orientated. Research work is at present being carried out to develop message-orientated examinations. In the meantime, the pupils' competence and effort in message-orientated communication during lessons should be reflected, through some form of continuous assessment, in terminal and sessional reports and total examination marks. This should apply to all the communicative skills exhibited by the pupils: understanding, speaking, reading and writing, at message-orientated levels.

Public examination, e.g. C.S.E. and 'O' level examinations, though still medium-orientated need pose no threat to pupils who have undergone this method of language learning. Experience has shown that pupils in the trial schools during the life of the Schools Council Project, fared far better than pupils taught by the same teachers before the Project was introduced. A close analysis of the various methodological steps involved in the classroom procedure should make it clear that pupils who have learnt to handle their world through the medium of Welsh on message-orientated levels, can quite easily cope with medium-orientated work, no matter whether this relates to school tests or public examinations.

CONCLUSIONS

Nobody expects that teachers will be able overnight to change from their normal teaching routines to the method described here. It is not merely that attitudes need to be changed; it is also necessary for new teaching skills to be developed. Language advisers, university departments of education and colleges of education should take upon themselves the tasks of helping teachers to bring about these changes. This ought to be a common effort, with the classroom teacher, as always, bearing the brunt. Some teachers already teach this way, but many others still find their tasks difficult, wearisome and largely unrewarding. The communicative way of teaching should not be considered a panacea for eliminating all difficulties. In many ways it shifts our difficulties from one area to another. Yet at least we cannot be accused by the public of not trying to help our pupils to receive a more rewarding and effective education.

Pupils already in secondary schools may also find it difficult to adjust themselves to new ways, though the difficulties encountered in this respect in our Project schools were minor and easily alleviated. For instance, in one Project school the following exchange was overheard between two pupils in the corridor on their way to a Welsh lesson: 'What have we got now?' . . . 'Red Indians!' It is when pupils begin to see their Welsh lessons in this light that one may say a breakthrough has occurred.

REFERENCES

Beardsmore, H. B. (Ed.), *Elements of Bilingual Theory,* (Study Series No. 6), Vreije Universiteit, Brussels, 1982.

Beaudoin, M. *et al.,* 'Bilingual Education: A Comparison of Welsh and Canadian Experiences', *The Canadian Modern Language Review,* vol. 37, 3, 1981.

Burstall, C., *Primary French in the Balance,* NFER, 1974.

Butzkamm, W. and Dodson, C. J., 'The Teaching of Communication: from Theory to Practice', *International Review of Applied Linguistics,* xviii, 4, 1980.

Commission for Racial Equality, *Ethnic Minority Community Languages: A Statement,* CRE, July 1982.

Cummins, J., *Bilingualism and Minority-Language Children,* OISE Press, The Ontario Institute for Studies in Education, Toronto, 1981.

Dodson, C. J., *Language Teaching and the Bilingual Method,* Pitman, London, 1967, 1972.

'FL Teaching and Bilingualism', *Cilt Reports and Papers,* 14, CILT, London, 1976.

'Towards Bilingual Education', Commission for Racial Equality/ Centre for Bilingual and Language Education Conference, Aberystwyth, 1982.

'Bilingualism, Language Teaching and Learning', Presidential Address, British Association for Language Teaching, *The British Journal for Language Teaching,* 1983.

Second Language Acquisition and Bilingual Development: a theoretical framework, *Journal of Multilingual and Multicultural Development*, 1985, forthcoming.

Dodson, C. J. and Price, E., *Bilingual Education in Wales: 5-11*, Evans/Methuen Educational/Schools Council, 1978.

Dodson, C. J., Price, E. and Williams, I. T., *Towards Bilingualism*, University of Wales Press, Cardiff, 1968.

Gittins Report, *Primary Education in Wales*, Central Advisory Council for Education (Wales), HMSO, 1967.

Hawkins, E., *Modern Languages in the Curriculum*, Cambridge University Press, 1981.

Littlewood, W., 'Role-performance and Language Teaching,' IRAL, 13, 1975.

Schools Council, Gweithgareddau i'r Plant Bach (Llawlyfr i'r Athrawes), 1975.

Trim, J. L. M., *Developing a European Unit/Credit Scheme of Adult Language Learning*, Pergamon Press, 1981.

Modern Languages 1971-1981, Council of Europe, Report presented by CDCC Project Group 4, with a resumé by J. L. M. Trim.